How to get a job in Grand Prix Racing

RICHARD LADBROOKE

Copyright © 2015 Richard Ladbrooke

All rights reserved.

ISBN: 9781520395289

CONTENTS

Foreword
Introduction
About the author
Disclaimers

Part 1 **Getting Started** Pg 8
How to use this guidebook
Before you start and setting realistic goals

Part 2 **What is it like to work in Formula 1?** Pg 14
A day in the life of Formula
Champagne and caviar
Monaco, Monza, Singapore & Silverstone
Money in Formula 1
What is the Formula 1 of tomorrow?

Part 3 **What sort of person works in F1 and what do they do?** Pg 36
A typical F1 team and the people who work in it
What job can I do in F1?
What are winners made of and do I have the right stuff?
What F1 wants from you - essential skills

Part 4 **School Days, University and Education** Pg 72
What to study, where and when
F1 in Schools and other education initiatives
University choices
The things that school cannot teach you
Get out, get involved, get in

Part 5   **The real secrets to a career in Formula 1**   Pg 115

There is no secret

Work placements and apprenticeships

F1 and how it fits within the motorsport industry

The racing ladder

Stepping stones - the simple secret

How to fail and what NOT to do

What can I expect in return - salaries & benefits

Ready for Formula 1

Part 6   **Essential Resources**   Pg 165

FOREWORD

Formula 1 is one of the most widely recognised sports in the world and is synonymous with technology, danger, glamour and most of all money. The sport is commonly believed to be the exclusive realm of international corporations and millionaires with iconic images of the harbour at Monaco as the backdrop to the exotic race machinery only serving to enforce this view. F1 however is one of the few global sports where perfectly ordinary people can take part through their everyday jobs and play a pivotal role in the outcome of each Grand Prix.

There are many thousands of engineers, mechanics and marketing people across the world who earn their living by working in F1 behind the scenes. They share in a bit of the excitement and glamour of the sport each day without having to be a global superstar or wealthy corporation owner. I am one of those ordinary people and this book intends to show you that you too can be a part of that extraordinary world.

This book came about not as my idea but from the persuasion of others, urging me to share what I knew about the industry and from telling me that someone should be providing advice and direction for those aspiring to work in Formula 1.

On more than one occasion I have been asked if I can help guide sons, daughters or pupils of close friends who want to work in Formula 1 when they have been unsure where to start. I have enjoyed seeing how much those people have benefitted from just a few simple pieces of advice and encouragement and several have gone on to have successful Formula 1 careers. Many people are capable of working in Formula 1 but are confused by the mystery and conflicting advice that is currently out there. Sadly, many of them miss out on the opportunity as a result of bad advice and that concerns me greatly.

Researching ideas for this book reminded me just how little real advice is available for aspiring Formula 1 people and it emphasised how little has changed since my own struggles to make it to F1, coming from a family with no history of motorsport.

As I formulated a set of recommendations in my mind I was encouraged to put my thoughts down and have them ready to share with others. In 2013, I started a blog at www.jobinf1.com where I wrote a collection of articles on various aspects of job searching and building experience relevant to working in motorsport. The response was amazing and now tens of thousands of people find that site each month to read through the content and ask me questions via the blog comments.

This book is the structured and organised result of all of that discussion and what I have taught others. I very much hope that you find it both useful and inspiring.

INTRODUCTION

Have you ever wanted to sit in a Formula 1 car on the starting grid at the Monaco Grand Prix? Have you ever wondered what it must be like to be part of the pit crew during a crucial Formula 1 tyre change? Have ever you dreamt of what it must be like to be allowed inside the F1 paddock or inside one of the ultra-high technology factories that produces Formula 1 cars?

If you have then you are not alone. Formula 1 is full of glamorous, high octane thrills and anyone who has a passion for speed will understandably want to get close to the action. The danger, noise, speed and competition are an adrenaline buzz which makes a Grand Prix Sunday afternoon compulsive viewing for Formula 1 fans. Imagining yourself on the grid and taking part in the action is all part of the lure that makes the sport so attractive.

These fantasies may excite but sadly they are experiences that few fans will ever get to fulfil. The cost of tickets is very high and even the best of those will not get you access to the teams and drivers. This type of privilege is usually the reserve of the sponsors, team owners and the mechanics and engineers who work for Formula 1 teams.

I am assuming that if you are reading this book then you are not a millionaire or a movie star. Unless you have won the lottery or have Hollywood at your fingertips then that lifestyle is probably also just a fantasy.

The unique thing about Formula 1 however is that you don't need to be any of those things in order to get the same access as the rich and famous. The television cameras might follow the movie stars and glittering celebrities but walking amongst them are some very ordinary people who just happen to have extraordinary jobs. I should know because I am one of them.

The engineers, mechanics and other members of a Formula 1 team are not rich or famous and yet they live a jet set lifestyle that takes them to Monaco, Singapore, Silverstone and Monza. They discuss set up and strategy with the fastest drivers in the world, design and assemble some of the most expensive cars ever made and influence the outcome of every Grand Prix. They make Formula 1 what is it and work so close to the action that they feel the heat of the tyres, smell the burning of the brakes and taste the champagne. It might sound like a fantasy world but there is no reason at all why <u>you</u> cannot be one of these people.

Combining a sport you love with the way you earn your living is a true privilege and allows those lucky enough to do it to indulge themselves in racing fantasies almost every day of the week. In my career, I have fired up V10 engines, been the gunman in pitstop practices and walked the starting grid of famous race tracks. I've helped to design cars which have won Grand Prix and casually chatted with World Champion drivers. This is certainly not fantasy, it is a reality that you can be an integral part of.

I don't wish to boast and that is not the purpose of this book. The truth is that I am not special, I am not unique and I am not even especially talented in what I do. The purpose of this book is to encourage you to believe that this life is not out of your reach and that it is not just pure fantasy. You too can make a career in Formula 1 from whatever starting point, background or pedigree you may come from. *Anyone* can work in Formula 1 if they so wish and I will show you how this is possible.

When I was trying to break into the sport myself, I found very little in the way of encouragement and advice about what I needed to do at school and how to gain vital experience. Several decades later and despite the invention of the internet not much seems to have changed.

I come from a family with no background in racing and when I decided that this was the career path that I wanted to follow my parents could not help me as it was well outside of their personal experience. Motorsport is a very different world to many other industries and one which is often misunderstood. At school, I received a great deal of conflicting advice and was told many times that I couldn't work in F1 and that I should pursue another more realistic career. Thank goodness I did not listen to those people.

When writing this book, I wanted to create a real resource that people could come to and find the encouragement and ideas they needed to follow their dreams of working in Formula 1. Much of the existing advice I have read on the internet is written by people who have never worked a day in Formula 1 and is seemingly full of contradiction and nonsense. This is just plain wrong.

Through this book I hope to pass on what I know about the Formula 1 industry and show you the qualifications, personal qualities and experience that the teams are looking for. I hope to show you how to see through the mystery that surrounds recruitment in F1 and where to find those elusive openings into the industry. I hope to encourage you, give you the confidence that you can make it and show you how to beat the masses to reach your goals. You don't need to be a genius to work in Formula 1 but you need to be smart about how you approach it.

I want this book to be the guide that I was desperate for as a 10 year old boy, one which will also give you the direction you need to have the same exciting career that Formula 1 has given me. I hope one day that you too can walk down that grid at Monaco and who knows we may even see each other there one day.

Good luck and I hope you enjoy it.

ABOUT THE AUTHOR

Richard Ladbrooke is a degree qualified engineer who has worked in Formula 1 and other forms of motorsport both in the UK and America for nearly two decades. He has seen top level motorsport from both the winner's podium and from the back of the grid.

Richard comes from a family wholly unconnected to motorsport and knew nothing about the sport when he began his own pursuit of a career in racing in the 1980's. He has forged his own way through this complex and competitive industry learning many difficult lessons along the way.

Richard has worked at a variety of Formula 1 teams, in a number of different roles and has observed how others achieve their success and what qualities an individual requires in order be a winner.

He is involved in the recruitment process within Formula 1 and takes an active interest in education and work experience for aspiring youngsters. As well as being a motor racing enthusiast he enjoys writing in his spare time and is keen to share his thoughts and ideas so that others can also have the chance the experience the privileges that he has enjoyed through his career.

DISCLAIMERS

This book is unofficial and is not associated in any way with the Formula One group of companies. F1, FORMULA ONE, FORMULA 1, FIA FORMULA ONE WORLD CHAMPIONSHIP, GRAND PRIX and related marks are trademarks of Formula One Licensing B.V.

It is also not associated with any team competing in the Formula 1 World Championship past, present or future and the purchase of this book should not be considered as any right of access or employment to any team or its confidential information. The views expressed in this book are solely those of the author and do not in any way represent his employer or any fellow competitor in Formula 1.

The recommendations given here do not guarantee any form of future employment whether in Formula One or any other industry. The author is not responsible for any success or failure as a result of following the guidance in this book. No responsibility for loss or damage to any person or company, by result of any person acting or refraining from action as a result of material in this publication can be accepted by the author.

The author is also not responsible for any loss, death or injury sustained as a result of any career or pursuit of any career in Formula One. It is entirely the responsibility of the reader to independently verify any information provided themselves before acting upon it.

Part 1 : Getting started

1 How to use this guidebook

If you have ever followed Formula 1 and especially if you have ever wondered how the people who work in the sport got to be in their enviable positions you will know that a veil of secrecy covers many things in Formula 1.

This book should not only provide you with practical advice and easy to follow recommendations to get a job in Formula 1 but it also attempts to demystify and educate about the motorsport industry and how it works.

The book is intended primarily for school or university students who are looking to make their career in Formula 1 and wish to know the educational routes and choices that will give them the maximum opportunity of working in the sport. Having said that, much of the advice is applicable at any stage of your career development and it is intended that you can pick up the book and benefit from it at any point along that journey.

For those who are already of working age it should still provide a useful guide as much of the advice is focussed around work experience and gaining skills in the workplace that are of value and attractive to Formula 1 teams. A key theme is the use of stepping stones and making the right job moves to manoeuvre yourself into Formula 1 from outside the industry.

The early chapters give you some background to the sport itself, the people who work in it and the jobs that they do. From that point you can focus on a specific role, the qualifications that you need to do it, the experience that teams will want to see on your application and the work history that can put you ahead of other applicants. Understanding the Formula 1 environment and how it works is the first stage in your success.

Attitude, work ethic and self-belief are essential skills and those qualities are discussed throughout the book. Developing those characteristics will help you to maintain focus on your goal even when inevitable setbacks occur and they still are important even when you finally break into the sport. Crucially I hope to teach you to see the openings into Formula 1 that others miss and to be ready to take advantage of them by having a wealth of relevant skills and experiences behind you even when you have never worked in F1 before.

The intention is to show you that there is no single path into F1 that each person must follow but that successful individuals will forge their own way through knowledge and understanding of the sport. I hope that through this book that I can encourage you to use these same qualities to develop your career and enjoy everything that top level motorsport has to offer. The opportunities are there and there is no reason why you should not be the person who benefits from them.

As a final note, I want to make it clear that the book will not write your job applications for you or give you tips for the interview. My intention is that through this book you will gain the confidence, knowledge and understanding of the industry so that you can take control of your career yourself. If you reach that stage, your success will then not just be down to luck or knowing the right people. If you follow my advice your eyes will be open to the inner workings of this sport and that will enable you to follow your own path to Formula 1.

2 Before you start and setting realistic goals

Formula 1 is a very competitive sport.

The relentless pursuit of success and the vast sums of money involved makes Formula 1 one of the most ruthless sporting environments in the world. Success is never guaranteed and even for those who do win, their reign at the top is likely to be short lived as another even more determined group will be racing up behind them to steal their glory. Formula 1 is not an easy place to exist.

Whilst the working environment for engineers, mechanics and marketing people may not quite be as cut throat as it is for the drivers there is no doubt that there are no free rides available in F1. The scenes that you see on television portray a world of glamour, success and excitement but underpinning all of that is a tremendous amount of blood, sweat and tears. To make Formula 1 happen takes a huge amount of hard work and you should be under no illusion that it is an easy career.

I truly believe that anyone can be successful in F1 as you do not have to be a rocket scientist or a brain surgeon to take part, contrary to popular belief. You do however need to be driven, competitive and prepared to stick at it even when things are not going well. My team would dearly love to win every race that we enter but the truth is that I and the majority of people who work in F1 do an awful lot more losing than winning. The satisfaction that you get from the good days is what keeps you motivated and working away through the bad days. The drive to keep pushing comes from the hope that someday you will get the pay back and it will be your turn to spray the champagne and stand on the top step of the podium.

Getting a job in F1 in the first place has exactly the same parallels. You should not expect to apply for the first job you see and be on a plane to Monaco the next weekend. The sport's popularity means that there is tremendous competition for what is a limited number of jobs and so you are competing against the many thousands of people who also want to make a career in racing. No matter how talented you are you should be preparing yourself for a potentially long process with setbacks and difficulties along the way. Nothing in this life is easy and this is especially so if the end goal is worthwhile.

When I first decided that I wanted to work in F1 I was around 10 years old and like many people I wanted first and foremost to be a racing driver. Whilst I had a modest attempt at making it behind the wheel it soon became clear that this was a step too far and that my future lay in the technical side of the sport. I had a very definite idea of what I wanted to do and even which team I wanted to work for. This was my motivation.

I am not afraid to tell you that I never made it into that job nor have I worked for my childhood fantasy team. My career has taken many twists and turns, not least taking me to the United States where I worked on the IndyCar scene for several years before returning to Europe and finally making it into F1. That move was never in my career plan but looking back now I would not change it for any reason. I had certain goals when I set out but first and foremost I just wanted to work in racing and it has been a fascinating journey along the way. I feel tremendously proud of what I have achieved in my career but I still set new goals and those goals are what keep me racing each year. Predicting the future is very difficult but adapting to the directions that life takes you in is all part of the process.

My point is that you should definitely have aspirations as these are what motivate us to get out of bed in the morning but you should be prepared for life to take you where you need to go. That place might be slightly different to the team or job that you dream about today but it does not mean that it is any less worthy than what you set out to do. As you learn about the industry and what working in Formula 1 is all about then perhaps you will see that you are best suited a role which you did not even know existed. The sport changes every year and so should you, adapting to the opportunities that come your way. The most important thing is to keep striving and moving forward.

I urge you to stretch for your dreams and use them to drive yourself forwards but to enjoy the journey as much as the end goal itself. Working in motorsport is a very special career and for fans of the sport (which is what we all are) it is simply a privilege. You might dream of being the technical director of Ferrari or a race engineer at McLaren but just get out there, get involved and see what happens.

I've worked in this sport for many, many years now but some days I still have to pinch myself and check that this is real. The buzz from working with the world's fastest cars and the world's best drivers is something that you cannot get from just any career. The smell of race fuel in the morning, the rattle of wheel guns and the deafening sound of an F1 engine at full throttle are the unmistakeable back drop to life in my office. I hope you find this book motivating and insightful and that it can help you along your own personal journey to success in Formula 1.

Part 2 : What is it like to work in Formula 1?

1 A day in the life of Formula 1

We have all seen the television pictures of the Monaco Grand Prix with the million dollar yachts in the harbour and the starting grid before the race full of royalty and Hollywood film stars. This is one of the world's most expensive sports in one of the world's most glamorous settings. The Monaco GP an iconic event and the TV images beamed into our homes are what typically define Formula 1 as a sport.

The danger, excitement, noise and money that go with Formula 1 all add up to create a tremendous attraction for fans and spectators but they also act as a lure for people who want to work in the sport and take part in one of these iconic events. Most of us at some point will have dreamt of being a racing driver, what it must be like to drive a Formula 1 car around the streets of Monaco and spray the champagne as the winner. It is a common fantasy but sadly not very many people will ever get the chance to experience it.

We might also have dreamt about what it must be like to be a member of a Formula 1 pit crew and to have the ability and skill to change all four wheels and tyres in a matter of seconds. The men and women who travel with the teams, talk with the drivers and design and build these amazing machines seem to have an incredibly envious position. A team shirt and paddock pass are a golden ticket and most fans would give their back teeth to spend even a day working for an F1 team. What is it really like to work in Formula 1?

Formula 1 races take place on around 20 weekends in a typical year and television broadcasts those events into millions of homes across the world. This is Formula 1 as most people know it but the sport exists for 365 days a year and not just on race weekends. The industry behind those images is rarely seen in comparison.

The races are packed full of speed and rivalry but that same competition exists away from the race track and back at the factories. In reality, those races are won and lost during the day to day business of Formula 1 and back at base is where the majority of ideas, decisions and advances are made.

RICHARD LADBROOKE

I have only ever briefly worked outside of motorsport and so this industry has been my day to day reality for as long as I can remember. I am well aware however that my working day is somewhat different to the majority of my friends and family. It's a cliché, but for myself and for the majority of my colleagues, working in Formula 1 is not just a job it's a passion. I don't think I would do it if it wasn't. It is certainly a somewhat unique place to be and I hope in this chapter to convey a little bit about what it means to work in this industry and what a typical day is like.

Racing is a strange thing. Take a step backwards and think about why we all do this. Is there really a great deal of point to it? We expend a huge amount of time, energy and money to essentially drive around in circles for 2 hours and see who wins. The winner gets to spray some champagne but the celebrations soon die down. We pack up, move on and do the whole thing again a few weeks later in a different country and quite possibly on the other side of the world. On paper at least, the effort required is really quite hard to justify against the end result.

Logically we should probably be spending our time doing something more noble and worthwhile. There are many terrible problems and far too much suffering in the world that need of our attention. The same effort and money that goes into Formula 1 could potentially help to alleviate some of these bigger issues.

For someone who doesn't understand or enjoy racing it is hard to see why I or anybody else would want to spend hour after hour and day after day making racing cars, especially when they see the stress that it can cause. On a purely rational level Formula 1 is just not worth the effort. It is perfectly possible to earn a living doing something less taxing and spend more time at home watching soap operas or doing crosswords. The vast majority of people you meet have chosen the latter.

If you are reading this book however you probably do not see the world this way. If you are anything like me, racing is something which holds a special and near addictive fascination for you. When it comes to racing, logic and reason are replaced by a competitive drive which goes well beyond the realms of rationality. I was always a quiet and studious child and not a particularly sporty one but discovering Formula 1 awoke a passion inside me which has remained undiminished for decades. This passion is what drives my work, it's why I get out of bed in the morning and what keeps me going when things get difficult. Formula 1 for me is definitely more than just a job and to be at your best in this industry I think it's essential for everyone to have a similar motivation beyond the need simply to earn a living.

I think it was Ron Dennis of McLaren that was quoted as saying that if his cars had not finished first and second in the Grand Prix on Sunday he would feel a physical pain when he woke up on Monday morning. That may be an extreme but there is nothing like losing to motivate you to get back to work and put the situation right. It may be illogical but the drug of winning is so motivating for some people that they will push themselves well beyond what is normal to achieve it. It is definitely not just a job.

I am far from alone in being motivated by racing and using my competitive drive in Formula 1. The vast majority of my team have the same attitude and put huge amounts of their energy and effort into the car and team performance. It's hard to be ambivalent in an industry like this and the collective energy of the team sweeps everyone along with it. It is a very different working environment to the majority of office or workshop jobs.

Imagine an environment where 500 similarly passionate people work towards a common goal. Your aim is simply to beat the other teams at the same game. Each one of those teams is made up of yet more driven individuals who are desperate only to do a better job than you do. It is amazing what can be achieved with a relatively small amount of people when a can do attitude and competitive drive prevails.

Racing creates an atmosphere of openness, invention and satisfaction that is simply none existent in most ordinary industries. It makes a real difference to go to work in an environment where the majority enjoy what they do and want to be there. There is very little red tape and bureaucracy in motorsport and day to day it is simply about getting the job done. Nobody is invisible in a Formula 1 team and right from day one you will be given responsibility and important work to do. It doesn't really matter who you are or where you came from. If you demonstrate that you can do something well you will be loaded up with work and quickly be given the opportunity to build a reputation. There is always more work than people in F1 so the more you can take on the more you will learn and the quicker you will build your experience. F1 is in many ways a very straightforward environment, there are no excess layers of management, grades or pay structures to get in your way. Your success and work environment will be exactly what you make of it.

Being part of a culture where standards are very high will inevitably lift your own game and your rate of learning and abilities will be pushed along with that. It may be daunting to work with highly talented and experienced individuals at first but F1 teams are generally very inclusive groups. You will soon absorb knowledge and understanding which will lift your own skills well beyond where you could have pushed yourself on your own. Rivalry and competition drives people within their own teams too and this leads to a very rewarding and creative environment in which to work. The goal of winning is something which motivates and rewards people well beyond the majority of ordinary jobs.

I tell new starters that you should fully expect to be thrown straight in the deep end and learn to swim for yourself. F1 is not known for putting its arm around you and helping you along and you should not expect to be put on a 2 year graduate programme or structured training course. Training in Formula 1 tends to be real and on the job in whatever the latest crisis happens to be that week. You will learn to swim quickly as you will be surrounded by skilled and experienced people who you can watch and absorb ideas and skills from.

F1 is an environment where you typically learn the hard way and opportunities and experiences come at you almost as fast as you can cope with. It will not take long before you are in the thick of it and doing the job like a seasoned veteran. The only thing that holds you back in F1 is your own work rate and ability to adapt. Formula 1 presents a fantastic opportunity for talented people to fulfil their potential as the open structure allows them to flourish.

The flip side of that open structure however is that there is often pressure. With trust comes responsibility and the knowledge that if you drop the ball and mess up your job then the impact will be felt across the team. It might be your dream to work on the pit crew and actually take part in the cut and thrust of an F1 race but this is a tough environment in which to work. Your mistakes might well be broadcast live on television for all to see, literally going up in smoke and costing the team a race win. This is the intensity of F1 and you should be prepared for that.

Even if you are not out there on the race team then you still have a critical role in competitiveness of the team. If you manufacture something that doesn't fit then the upgrade that you were working on might not make it to the next race and the team will fall behind in the development race. If a part that you designed breaks when your car is 20 seconds in the lead YOU will feel the responsibility. When you next see an F1 car broken down by the side of the road, give a bit of thought to the poor souls who are responsible for that and the pressure that they feel. There are very few jobs when your successes and failures are broadcast across the world but this is the nature of motorsport. Everything you do is at the sharp end win or lose.

The racing season may end in November but competition in Formula 1 is relentless. The race behind the scenes does not stop even though the chequered flag has fallen. Development is a year round occupation and there is rarely a chance to put your feet up and relax. If you take your foot off the gas then you can be sure your rivals will keep pushing and try to leave you behind. It is truly a race without end and you need stamina to stay in the game.

Simply getting the cars and equipment from one race to the next requires an astonishing amount of work which is often unseen. As soon as the flag falls the mechanics are packing up spares, tools and equipment ready for freight to the next event. Back at the factory replacement parts and upgrades are being packed to rendezvous with the race team and the designers are already dreaming up new parts for races later in the season. It's a cliché but if you standstill in Formula 1 you go backwards.

Working in Formula 1 is rarely dull or boring. Nothing ever stays still for long. A breakdown or an accident at a race can cause a crisis which needs to be fixed as soon as humanly possible and a race against time exists to get the solution ready in time for the next race.

It has often been said that Formula 1 is about constant crisis management and rarely is a team comfortable or on top of everything that it needs to do. Your work in Formula 1 is never done and each day that you go to work you never really know what you will be working on. Friends and family often have this image that what I do involves a great deal of deep thinking, research and head scratching. Believe me, you need to think a great deal but the best people in motorsport think on their feet and it is urgency that that defines most days. The way I describe my job to people is to imagine that you have 10 things to do at the same time and they all needed to be finished yesterday. As soon as you have finished one of them, another task appears and so it goes on.

A typical day in a Formula 1 is one of controlled chaos, many things happening at once and constant change. The ability to work under pressure is so important in this type of environment and this where personality rather than academic ability take over. How you handle pressure and chaos is normally a good measure of your performance and not something that you naturally learn at school. Experience teaches you how to deal with difficult situations and as we will see throughout this book, real world challenges and the skills that are gained from them are as important for your career development as qualifications and school. When you apply for a job in Formula 1 you are not only trying to convince the guy or girl on the other side of the table that you are academically qualified for the job but more often you need to convince them that you can cope with pressure and that they will be able to rely on you when things get difficult. If you take one thing from this book it should be the need to balance your school and academic learning with real world experience.

Playing with toy cars is the typical pastime of many little boys (and girls) and although they might hesitate to admit it, it's a love that many of them never grow out of. The popularity of television programmes like Top Gear would suggest that fast cars still hold a fascination for many adults, they just happen to cost a lot more than the toy cars they played with as children.

When working in Formula 1 you are essentially being paid to play with fast cars. Forget the hard work, the bare facts are that you are spending your time trying to make a fast car go faster and earning a living from it. There is something quite primal about working in racing. Aside from being an astronaut or actually being the driver, this is as close as you can get to acting out a childhood dream.

The budget of a Formula 1 team allows you to indulge in that dream too. If you have an idea, a desire to try something new then you have the right money, machines and exotic materials at your disposal. If you've ever wanted to upgrade your own car with big brakes, more power and wings and spoilers, now you can do that for real and at a very sophisticated level. In many cases your imagination and the rule book are the only compromises. It's very rare in life that you get to indulge yourself in quite this way but a Formula 1 team is about as close as you can get to being an engineer's and mechanic's playground. V8 engines, regenerative turbos, slick tyres, carbon brakes and pitstop practice are the vocabulary of your working day and you can discuss, debate and argue about Formula 1 matters to your heart's content. If you are the kind of person who cannot get enough of Formula 1 then this is the dream work environment for you.

Don't get me wrong however, working in F1 is not a game it is a serious business. There is always time for a laugh and a joke but whatever it is that you are working on needs to show results sooner or later or the competitiveness of the sport will catch and overtake you. You are given all the tools and freedom to pursue what you want to work on and how you want to do it but you need to perform and produce the goods. The work is never done and even if you make improvements then you need to produce more of it and better what you have done already. This is the constant nature of racing and the continuous improvement that it demands. This is the essence of the game and what the job is all about. For someone who enjoys racing and fast cars there can be few jobs that provide the satisfaction and fast paced turnover of work and results that Formula 1 does. It truly is a playground for Formula 1 addicts.

For all of the love of working, what each of us really wants is to be a winner. Where F1 differs from so many other professions is the way in which you get feedback from what you have done in your day to day role. In F1 we don't need to wait for end of year accounts or sales figures and we don't have to rely on our boss to tell us how the department is doing against our competitors. Our results are played out on television and in the news every 2 weeks for everyone to see and the feedback is very direct. The immediacy of that feedback is one of the unique aspects of working in F1.

Whether you are a designer, mechanic or marketing person, the work that you do is very visible and you see exactly what you have been working on come to fruition. Imagine you have been negotiating with a new sponsor, working hard behind the scenes to persuade them that they need to get on board and come and join the team. You've worked on branding and colour schemes, some launch ideas and driver events to get the maximum value for them and to provide the budget that your team needs to get to the next level of competitiveness. When your car lines up on the grid with that sponsor branding on it and your drivers are interviewed with that sponsor's logo emblazoned on their race suits you will get an amazing sense of satisfaction that you were instrumental in bring them on board. The results of your labour and your efforts are visible for everyone to see.

The pinnacle however is always seeing the car you have worked on achieving success on track. I am fortunate in that some of the cars I have worked on have won races and world championships. I can't take sole responsibility for that obviously but even the small part that I played in those successes gives me an incredible feeling of satisfaction and achievement. It's something that I dreamt of when I was trying to break into the sport and having done it I am no less proud of the fact. It is something I can tell my children and grandchildren about one day and show them the photos and the trophies.

The world of F1 often seems like an impenetrable fortress from the outside and there were many, many days where I felt despair and frustration because my dreams felt so far away. Sticking at it however I managed to break down those barriers and seeing my car crossing that line to win a Grand Prix was all the reward that I needed for the hard work. It was worth all that effort. I hope through this book that I can motivate you to believe that you too can get involved in the sport and experience that feeling of winning a Grand Prix and perhaps even winning a world championship. It may seem a long way away today and just a distant dream but I can assure you that anyone can achieve it. The day to day reality of working in this industry is something very unique that I would recommend to anyone who loves Formula 1. It is far from an ordinary job.

In the following chapters I will show you the detailed steps that you need to follow and some of the secrets of the industry which can get you ahead of the pack and fulfil those dreams. I am certain that if you wish to, then you too can be a Grand Prix winner.

2 Champagne and caviar

Formula 1's image is all about glamour, technology and sophistication.

It breeds on exclusivity, preserving itself as the realm of the super-wealthy and the well connected. The paddock club of any Formula 1 race is populated by successful, beautiful and powerful people who must seem (and often are) like movie stars to the average Formula 1 fan. The apparent division breeds contempt but it is also a large part of the appeal of F1 for many viewers. After all, how many people would watch the grid walkabout of the Monaco Grand Prix if it were open to your next-door neighbour and nerdy car fanatics rather than George Clooney and Jennifer Lawrence? I suspect not many.

This division and this exclusivity is all part of a very deliberate plan. F1 often talks about wanting to be more "fan friendly" but I think that something aspirational about F1 needs to be maintained, at least on television. Formula 1 always has and always will be about high spending and it is marketed very carefully to maintain the appearance of being the playground of the elite and highly important players. Access is great in theory but real fascination is based on fantasy and aspiration and so F1 must appear to keep itself just out of reach.

This shroud of exclusivity adds to the mystique but it is also largely the reason why a career in F1 seems so difficult to get. I have heard several people tell me that you need to be rich and well connected to work in F1 but this is thankfully not true. Such an impression comes simply from mixing up the fantasy with the reality. The key thing to remember is that employment in F1 is much more accessible than it appears and is something quite separate to the movie star exclusivity that is portrayed by the TV coverage. I hope to show you why and how to breakthrough those barriers in the following chapters.

A clique of champagne and caviar is what people most commonly associate with Formula 1 aside from the speed and the ever present danger. An untouchable world of luxury creates jealousy amongst average people which becomes even more readily apparent when they find out that you work in the sport. For them, it is obvious that you must spend your weekends going to cocktail parties and driving model girlfriends around in supercars.

I hate to be a disappointment but this isn't the case.

The high class luxury of Formula 1 entertainment does not stretch to the team members themselves. Well, not often. If you are motivated to work in the sport because you believe that you can gain access to this kind of enviable lifestyle then you may need to think again. Working in F1 is certainly a privilege in many ways but you will not spend your working day drinking expensive wines and nibbling on canapés unless you are a current or potential team sponsor. You can earn a very good living in Formula 1 but before we go further we need to separate the fantasy from the reality.

The majority of F1 people are very ordinary. They drive ordinary cars and they have ordinary friends. They just happen to work in an extraordinary environment. The environment of the team factory or even the pit garage is very different from that of the paddock club or the yachts in the Monaco harbour.

It is important to know that the vast majority of F1 workers rarely go to a Grand Prix. This may come as a disappointment but it is the reality. The team that you see on the television comprises a very small part of the group that makes up the overall F1 team. Racing is only the tip of the iceberg and the bulk of a true Formula 1 team lies beneath the surface, working back at the factory to design the next upgrade to the car and watching the race on television. These people are the F1 ordinary, of which I am one.

This is a point that many people find difficult to take in but it is key to understanding the type of work that people in a Formula 1 team actually do. I have worked in F1 for many years but friends and family still express surprise when I answer the door or phone on Grand Prix weekends. "Shouldn't you be in Brazil?" is a typical question, or "I thought you were meant to be in Singapore?" I have been to quite a few Grand Prix during my career but I, like the vast majority of F1 people have a job role which normally has nothing to do with running the car at race weekends.

The racing part of Formula 1 is actually very small compared to the task of designing, developing and manufacturing a Grand Prix car. A Formula 1 team should be thought of as an engineering company which also runs a racing team rather than the other way around. I'll go into job roles in more detail later in this book but the vast majority of F1 people work a 9 to 5 type role at the factory and go home at the weekends. It is very ordinary. Their work is in designing, manufacturing, testing, inspecting or assembly of the various parts that make up the car. It is fulfilling work but it certainly isn't as glamorous as the television might make you think.

A typical F1 person is far more likely to live in or near to the town or village where their team is located rather than in Monte Carlo or Singapore. They are more likely to be walking their dog or having a pint at their local pub at weekends than they are to be sipping champagne in a harbour yacht. It is a world away in terms of lifestyle.

Hopefully this revelation doesn't come as a surprise to you. You might be disappointed to hear that F1 is in most cases very down to earth and ordinary but I hope that you actually see it as very good news. It is good news because it should convince you that F1 is accessible, it is for ordinary people like you and I and that it is within your grasp. F1 is a sport ruled by money and expense but it does not use that as a barrier for entry for those of us who work in the sport. Two very different worlds collide on a Grand Prix weekend and it is important to be able to separate them and focus on which one it is that you are trying to be a part of. If you want to be a millionaire or a movie star then I'm afraid that I don't have the answers for you.

Having told you just how ordinary day to day life in F1 can be, it does not mean that there is no glamour whatsoever. Some very extraordinary things occur in F1 and there is an overlap of every day activity with events that remind you that you work in one of the world's most spectacular sports.

An "ordinary" day at work might well be disturbed by the arrival in the office of Lewis Hamilton and his entourage or by a television camera crew wishing to film for an upcoming broadcast. Sponsors and other guests might be having a factory tour and be shown round your office or assembly area and you might even have to do a brief talk to explain what you do or something about the parts which you are working with.

A team's drivers visit the factory at regular intervals and will often mingle with the workforce to have a general chat or to find out a little bit more about what is happening. You might even end up parking next to them in the car park and walking in with them to reception. Most teams don't segregate their canteens and so it's perfectly possible to sit down to lunch with a world champion and find out a little bit more about them. Many teams have company gyms and it's not uncommon to see a driver in there at lunch time lifting weights or using a running machine. Should you work in the simulator or customer facing areas of the factory you might even be on first name terms with them.

At the circuit is where you see the merging of the two faces of Formula 1 most closely and it is here that you are most likely to experience the moments of glamour that working in Formula 1 has to offer. The first time you get issued with your team gear and a paddock pass is a very special day and although they may deny it, everyone who goes trackside in F1 gets a buzz out of wearing it. It's the first time that you truly feel part of the show and you will see the envy and jealously of passers-by as they wish they were in your place. It's something that I will never forget and one of those feelings of fulfilment that I will carry with me in later life.

Since parc ferme rules were introduced following qualifying on Saturday afternoons, the work load for team members on Saturday night and Sunday morning has been dramatically reduced. The cars cannot be adjusted or rebuilt before the race start apart from essential maintenance that must be carried out before an FIA delegate. This means that most of the guys get out for a beer or two and depending on the venue there are often large organised parties where team members get VIP access. Party cities such as Montreal, Austin and Melbourne put on a great show but it is Monaco where the real celebrations start. Huge yachts such as the Red Bull energy station and Force India's Indian Empress host exclusive parties which invite team members as well as movie stars, models and politicians. It's a place where everyday life is left behind and you can experience a whole difference existence. Just don't wake up in the morning expecting it to continue!

F1 is certainly not a 24 hour party and you should not be motivated simply by the desire to live a glamorous lifestyle. You should be prepared for most of your working existence to be rather more normal and down to earth. Reminders that this business is extraordinary will never be far away though. If you work in F1 for long enough you will no doubt experience some extraordinary things and live the high life even if it is just for the day. It's all part of the experience and the special appeal of Formula 1 which I hope I can help you be a part of though the remaining chapters of this book.

3 Monaco, Monza, Singapore & Silverstone.

For all of the interest, sophistication and technology that is evident at the factory there is no doubt that most people are interested in working in F1 because of the racing. With races taking place across the globe and in some very beautiful and glamorous settings there is an undeniable attraction to the idea of being part of this travelling circus. The thought of spending your working life being paid to do something you might otherwise have to buy a ticket to go and watch seems too good to be true. It certainly beats the idea of a dull and repetitive office job.

A Formula 1 car at full speed is still something of awe to me even though I have been doing this job for years and it is at the racetrack where F1 truly comes to life. Modern TV coverage is very good but it cannot convey the atmosphere, sound and smells of Formula 1 to match the experience of actually being there. To be in the pit lane and in an F1 garage is to be right at the heart of that action and it is something that any F1 fan should experience at least once. Sadly, it is an experience that money cannot buy unless you are a wealthy sponsor or a team employee. I can't help you with the first of those but the second is very possible and is the prime reason why I have written this book.

Working for an F1 team allows you access to all of this hidden world and there is no doubt that the first time you get to go to the track you will be grinning from ear to ear. To be in this environment is a true privilege and is an unforgettable experience for any fan of the sport. It is a completely unique way to experience F1 and will show you a different side to the sport which you probably have not appreciated until now.

From the garage, you can watch and take part in everything that is required to run one of these cars for a race weekend, listening to the driver talk about how the car performs on track and all of the strategy discussion that takes place on the team radio. The amount of radio chatter that takes place even for one team is difficult to keep up with such is the complexity and number of decisions that take place all of the time that the car is running. It is not uncommon for teams to have more than 10 radio channels of simultaneous conversation about setup, tyres, weather, data analysis and communication back to the factory. Only the race engineer talks to the driver and he/she must filter all of this information as the session goes on and pass on only that which is absolutely necessary. It is a high pressure environment and a very busy place to work but a fascinating way to watch a race!

Working in the pit garage or on the pit wall is another added dimension compared to watching from the spectator area. Being so close to the action you can actually smell and feel the heat from the car which is totally unique. After a qualifying run the car will be raging hot and the smell of sticky rubber, burning carbon brakes and bodywork will soon fill the garage. Mix this with fuels, oils and the adrenaline of competition and it is not hard to see why working for a Formula 1 team can be so addictive. This is no ordinary office environment.

As most of you will know, F1 races always take place on Sundays. Typically, a TV viewer will tune in for around 2 hours to watch the some of the build-up, the race itself and then perhaps the podium ceremony. They may watch some of the post-race interviews too, before going back to do whatever else they choose to fill their weekends with. It's a nice way to spend an afternoon but it is somewhat different to being at the race and having to work for a living.

F1 race meetings last for 3 days starting with free practice on Friday mornings (or Thursday in Monaco) and running over several sessions until the race on Sunday afternoon. If you travel with an F1 team however your race weekend will last much longer than that. Travel and preparation take as long if not longer than the race meeting itself.

For long haul races the mechanics and setup crew will typically fly out on the weekend preceding the race. Freight may have been sent a few days earlier still. Once on location each pit garage, motor home and hospitality unit must be setup well before any track action takes place and before sponsors and guests arrive. Once that is done you have yet to build the car and have it scrutineered. This preparation process is meticulous in itself and may be delayed by parts shortages or bodywork modifications to take account of the latest upgrades. You can expect to be tired even before the first practice session starts.

Even after the chequered flag has fallen the cars must be legality checked, weighed, photographed and then at least partially stripped to check for damage or cracks before being readied for transport. The garage must also then be dismantled and packed away ready to ship to the next race. Add in the travel to these far flung places and it is not hard to see why an F1 race event can last for over a week rather than just a few hours on a Sunday afternoon. With jet lag and late nights at the track you will need some stamina to keep this up for whole a season and perform at your best.

You will often hear people casually tell you that F1 is not a job and that it is a way of life. Sometimes there will be a positive spin put on this and sometimes it will be negative. There is no doubt that doing a full season of F1 is a brilliant experience and will give you many memorable moments and experiences. It certainly is a way of life and might be the envy of your family and friends. You'll be in Monaco, Monza, Singapore and Silverstone, right at the centre of everything that makes F1 so special. It isn't everybody who has Fernando Alonso on speed dial on their mobile phone after all.

At the same time however a full season of F1 is very long, and takes up much of your precious spare time. The race season is now 19 races and if you work on the race team and your best friend decides to get married on a race weekend you cannot just take time off to go along and be the best man or bridesmaid. You have committed to the race team and need to accept that this jet set lifestyle will come at a cost. Even grabbing a few days holiday mid-season can be difficult as there is work to do back at the factory as well as at the race track. Towards the end of the year you are very likely to tire of airports, minibuses, hire cars and checking into and out of hotels. For a holiday you will probably just want to stay at home.

At the races you might be in a different country but the inside of the garage always looks the same and there isn't a huge amount of time for sightseeing! Great as it sounds this is not a job that suits everyone especially once the novelty has worn off and you are in your third or fourth season on the merry-go-round.

Very few people regret going racing but as a career you need to think carefully about whether it is for you. I hope through this book to convey what the reality is like, not just the fantasy. It is not uncommon for people to go racing for a few seasons but long term they will want to get back to the factory for a more ordinary existence as a designer or a technician. This is perfectly normal, but is something you should think about even before you start as the door back is not always open just when you need it. Ironically getting off the race team can be as difficult as getting on it in the first place. Whatever you chose to do, being on the road is certainly something to remember, something to tell others about and something to savour as a life experience. It is far from a normal work day experience and is an opportunity not to be missed for any fan or enthusiast of Formula 1.

4 Money in Formula 1

To many people, Formula 1 simply means money. If you ask the average person in the street what Formula 1 is all about then it is highly likely that their answer will in some way mention money. Money makes the world go round as the saying goes and that is never more true than in Formula 1.

Motor racing has always been expensive. In the 50's and 60's many of the teams were run by wealthy amateurs or 'gentlemen racers' as they were known. For them F1 was little more than a hobby and even though the cost of competing was considerably less than it is now this was no ordinary man's playground. As sponsorship was introduced and as the global reach of the sport has increased over the past decades, the income into the sport has increased accordingly and thus the cost of competition has increased even further.

Motor racing is different to most sports. In football you can put coats down to form goal posts and hone your skills in your back garden or on the school playing field. You need very little other than a ball and an appropriate pair of shoes to take part.

Even tennis or athletics are little different. Here the quality of the equipment you use will affect your performance and it may cost money to get access to a private court or running track but that cost is rarely prohibitive. Spending millions on the latest tennis racquet will not gain you a substantial advantage over a competitor.

In motor racing however just getting to the starting grid can cost a fortune. The initial outlay for an appropriate vehicle plus the cost of consumable items like tyres, fuel and repairing damage can very quickly add up to tens of thousands of pounds even in an entry level formula. You are never quite sure whether you are losing because you aren't driving well enough or whether someone richer than you has an extra advantage from outspending you. This is true from karting through to F1 and is an inherent part of the sport.

How much does Formula 1 cost ? This is a question that I've heard countless times but I'm yet to come up with the answer. The fact is that it is impossible to say. You cannot put a price on an F1 car or what it costs to compete. It may cost $1 million to manufacture a car (a number I plucked out of the air) but it may have cost ten times that much to develop the ideas and technology that go into producing that car so you could argue that the cost is potentially $11 million. If team B spends twice as much on developing their car as team A does then the material cost of that car is almost irrelevant because the development spend is the dominant expense. Two cars can sit on the grid but the money spent to put them there can be vastly different. The more appropriate question therefore is to ask how much it costs to *compete* in Formula 1.

The fact is that you can spend whatever you like in F1, within reason. Unlike tennis or football there is always more advantage to be gained from producing a faster and more technologically advanced car and so teams will spend as much as they need to in order to compete. If someone else comes along and spends more to produce a technologically more advanced car then everyone else will have to dig deeper into their own pockets and spend more to stay in the race. The only limit to spending will be how much they can raise through sponsor or investor income and only those partners can decide when the benefit of being involved in F1 exceeds the expenditure. Teams spend whatever cash they raise through sponsorship so the actual "cost" of F1 is more closely related to its commercial revenue and success than it is to the cost of physically making a car. The problems arise only when expenditure starts to exceed income or rather when ambition exceeds ability and results.

The Red Bull team has spent a huge amount of money in F1 over the past decade. It is one of the main components of the huge marketing machine that has turned Red Bull from an obscure energy drink into one of the most well known and easily recognised brand names in the world. I've heard it said that to create the same level of exposure and positive brand association through traditional TV or print advertising would have cost many times what the company has spent on F1.

The link between Red Bull and extreme or dangerous sports is ingrained in the psyche of its consumers and would be very difficult to create by another means. For Red Bull, the benefits of F1 are huge and the sport is actually cheap compared to alternative forms of advertising. The cost of F1 to the Red Bull parent company is only the amount that has been required to outspend and beat its rivals and it is likely that it could easily spend more and still find F1 to be a cost effective method of promotion.

Detractors and even hard-core fans often criticise Formula 1 for being more about business than sport but it is an inescapable fact that money is an essential component of motor racing. It is an emotive subject but it is also what creates part of the fascination surrounding the sport.

Unless you are a driver or team owner however, the cost of competition is not something that directly concerns you. With an ordinary job in Formula 1 there is no cost to the individual and in fact a job in F1 is a job like any other where you get paid a weekly or monthly salary to pay your bills. There is no cost of competition here and you are hired and compensated purely on your ability and experience.

Working in F1 however you will get to see first hand where a lot of the big money goes and it can sometimes be a strange feeling to deal with vast sums of money for what is essentially just two racing cars going around in circles. The expense for even relatively ordinary items can be eye watering.

In the good times, you can enjoy an unrivalled playground where money seems no object. Your working environment is ultra modern and equipped with everything you need to do a first class job. It's a privilege to be trusted with such vast sums of money and to be allowed to use it to develop your own ideas and desires. In no other industry are you given such free reign for your work and such a plentiful budget to make it work. F1 is mercifully free of the constraints of middle management and paperwork. It's a feature of working in F1 that you will be trusted with responsibility from the very beginning. You will be asked to solve problems and create solutions in the way that you want to, using the resources that you need.

The high stakes of F1 mean that success also comes with massive reward and as we will see later, that works its way into the pockets of everyone in the team. Without layers of management typical of other industries, the contribution of individuals is very visible in Formula 1 and if you make a success of your area or responsibilities it will be seen, appreciated and recognised. If you contribute to the team's success you will be rewarded appropriately. There is no doubt that you can make good money in F1 but we'll talk about that in a little more detail later.

Success is fantastic but as I have already alluded to, there can only one winner and the facts are that the majority of teams in F1 spend more time losing than winning. In the bad times the cost of F1 can be crippling, and many teams in the recent and distant past have failed to keep up and have fallen by the wayside. Job security is never guaranteed in any industry but F1 is less stable than many ordinary careers and this is something you should be prepared for.

Losing can also be very frustrating and if you are a competitive person then the success or failure of your team can often affect your mood and feelings of satisfaction. Many Sunday evenings have passed in silence in my house whilst I fume over lack of pace or inability of our drivers to keep their cars on the road for the duration of a Grand Prix. You live and breathe Formula 1 and if it doesn't go well it can get you down.

I have had many discussions with friends and family about whether the cost of F1 is justifiable and whether the whole sport is simply a waste of resources that could be better spent pursuing a more noble cause. At times, I have wondered the same but Formula 1 is entertainment and it brings a great deal of pleasure to many people worldwide. Ignoring the nuts and bolts of the cars, the cost is only very moderate compared to the spending power of many other corporations and the teams themselves are actually incredibly efficient organisations. The technology that is developed by these small groups of people can improve the emissions, safety and cost of everyday road cars all over the world. Materials and assembly methods developed in Formula 1 have also gone on to provide benefits to other high technology sectors.

Money is a continuous feature in F1 and any form of motorsport and you will see every side of it from greed and waste to profit and loss. You personally do not need to be rich or privileged to work within the sport. My hope is that this book will provide you with the advice and insight to allow you to do what you love for a career and at least earn a decent living in the process.

One of the key aims over the next few chapters is to help you understand how to build yourself as a commodity and gain the skills and experiences that F1 teams will value. Armed with this knowledge, you will then be able to not only make a career in F1 but also demand the sorts of salary and retainer that you might expect of such a high spending and high technology sport. Nothing in Formula 1 is ever easy but there is no doubt that the rewards for winning are very high and you can have you share of the spoils if you can prove yourself in this arena.

Part 3 of this book is concerned with how to build that experience and make yourself attractive to the teams to start your journey up the racing ladder.

5 What is the Formula 1 of tomorrow?

Formula 1 has changed a great deal since the early days of the championship in the 1950's and 60's. Not only have the cars become more technically advanced in that time but the drivers and teams have also become far more professional and well organised. Commercially the sport is now a true global phenomenon and aside from football it ranks as one of the most popular sports worldwide. Despite a recent global economic downturn, Formula 1 has continued to extend its reach and has phased in a brave new era with energy efficient V6 turbo engines which pave the way for great advances in the fuel efficiency of everyday road cars. In many ways F1 is now unrecognisable from the amateur sport that took to the circuit at Silverstone in May 1950 and is likely to be very different again 10 years from now.

The advances and changes that F1 has gone through however have also come at a cost. Critics will tell you that F1 is no longer a sport at all but that it is now simply a business. You will hear that all remnants of sportsmanship and fair play have long since vanished. I am not sure that I agree 100% with that but there is no doubt that commercial pressures in the sport make it a ruthless environment in which to do business. Some changes have been for the better and others for the worse but one thing I am certain about is that many more people earn a living through this sport now than have done at any previous time in history. It may not satisfy the purists but for someone wanting to make a career in F1 there has probably never been a better time to get involved.

Like it or loathe it, Formula 1 is a sport that never stands still. The racing competition is such that if you don't adapt to keep up with the latest developments then you will rapidly go backwards and the sport itself is similar in many ways. The Formula 1 of 2025 is very unlikely to look like the F1 of today but predicting what that sport will be like at that time is extraordinarily difficult. If I knew what was going to make an F1 car go quickly in 10 years' time then I would be designing and racing that car today and most likely winning the championship by a considerable margin.

Recent trends however indicate that the sport is changing in a number of ways that are likely to continue for the foreseeable future. In the 1980's and 1990's the number of races in each year was very stable at 16 per season but that number seems to be steadily growing as F1 taps into new and emerging markets worldwide. Looking at the hugely successful NASCAR series in the US which has 36 races per year there is room to expand if the logistics of global travel can keep up. My prediction is that F1 will have up to 25 races a year by 2025 and that teams may use 2 alternating sets of race crews to cover each event. The fatigue of a single season at today's levels is at the natural limit for many people and a support or relief crew will be required to meet any additional demand. This would mean that more jobs would be available in the race teams but they may come at the expense of some of the research and development roles back at the factory.

In the late 1980's there was a big increase in the number of teams attempting to qualify for Formula 1 races albeit of varying quality. New teams seemed to pop up every year and disappear again almost as quickly. At that time, it was possible to buy a stock Cosworth engine and put a car together with only a handful of skeleton crew and make it to the back of the grid. Some of the outfits were very unprofessional and the embarrassing exploits of the MasterCard Lola team in the late 1990's finally convinced the sport's rule makers to introduce the 107% qualification rule which allowed the stewards of the meeting to prevent a car from starting the race if it failed to set a time within 107% of the pole position. This rule enforced a minimum standard befitting the pinnacle of motorsport but has also meant that very few new teams have been able to make the leap from lower formulas up to the premier category. Between 1997 and 2010 there were remarkably few new entrants into Formula 1 other than the high spending Toyota team which ultimately withdrew after having failed to make significant progress towards winning.

2010 saw the FIA open up 4 new slots on the grid after the economic downturn led to the withdrawal of several of the high profile manufacturer teams. The USF1 team never made the grid and the Spanish backed HRT team rarely got off the back row before folding for good at the end of their second season. Caterham and Marussia survived longer but it seems now that neither of them will continue either, at least not in their current form. Developing a new team is certainly not easy but there seems an inevitable move towards encouraging more cars onto the grid and having greater diversity of competition.

Gene Haas has had an application accepted to form a completely new US based F1 team for entry in 2016 and there are rumours that at least one more new team is being put together in the background. Ultimately, I believe that F1 will almost certainly have more cars on the grid in the future than it does now, however those cars might be brought about. The Haas F1 team will be heavily backed by Ferrari and will purchase as much of the Ferrari car as the current rules will allow. Despite resistance from the purists I think future diversity is most likely to come in this form as customer cars allow a larger manufacturer team such as Ferrari or Red Bull sells its chassis and drivetrain to a smaller outfit. The new team can then develop it from that baseline package and rebrand the car with its own sponsors and team identity. Inevitably that team will still require a substantial technical budget to compete but having bought the essential component parts to get it up and running it will have saved considerable design and manufacturing costs. The cost of entry will be lower for all concerned.

There is considerable resistance to customer teams from many of the smaller midfield outfits as they see it as unjust and unfair. This comes from the fact that it would be possible for an entirely new entrant to Formula 1 to come along and buy a Ferrari or a Red Bull at a fraction of the development cost that Williams spend producing their machine for example and very quickly be able to compete with and beat them. Arguably this is unfair or an uneven playing field but teams such as Force India are already purchasing complete drivetrains (engine, gearbox and parts of the rear suspension) from competitor teams and using them to good effect. These arrangements allow the midfield teams to compete with larger and more technically advanced rivals by freeing up remaining resource and budget to further performance elsewhere. Where to draw the line seems to be the only current argument.

More teams would essentially mean more jobs and opportunities which is what we all want to hear. Customer teams would by definition be smaller than the manufacturer teams but more cars will always mean more jobs and a stronger jobs market. Ultimately the number of jobs in the F1 industry is only limited by the overall commercial success of the sport and how much revenue it can generate. How that revenue is distributed and how much exposure can be given to each investor/sponsor in the sport is the only real question but in my mind but more competition should make for more exciting sport and therefore greater viewing figures.

F1 needs to decide its own future and what it wants to be. The sport is currently going through a period of significant change and debate but ultimately, I see a bright future for Formula 1. The excitement, challenge and interest in high speed motor racing is a fundamental passion of so many people around the world that those who work in the sport will want to continue to produce cars and competition that fulfil that appetite in whatever form. Teams and manufacturers know that sport can be harnessed as a great force for change and so inevitably motorsport will be at the centre of automotive technology for many decades to come.

Part 3 : What sort of person works in F1 and what do they do?

1 A typical F1 team and the people who work in it

Understanding Formula 1 is one of the keys to working in Formula 1. The more you know about how the F1 business works the easier it will be for you to find the opportunities and openings that you need to develop your career in Formula 1. Understanding the F1 teams is what this particular chapter is all about.

Many, many people will tell you that they would like to work in F1. Ask them specifically which job they want to do in F1 however and many them will struggle to answer. General responses such as "I don't mind as long as I get to go the Grand Prix" or "I want to work with the drivers" are not uncommon but if you are serious about making a career in F1 then you need to know which job you want to do and then specifically target the qualifications, experience and career path that will get you there. With a clear target in mind you will be much more likely to succeed than if you meander along without specific direction. This chapter is all about helping you understand how a typical team is structured and what role each person plays within that.

The first thing to say is that all kinds of different people work in F1. Adrian Newey may be the design genius behind so many winning F1 cars of recent years but you don't need to be like him to work in F1. Contrary to what many people will tell you, you definitely DON'T need a PhD to work in Formula 1.

Success takes all kind of skills and talents and some of the most respected employees in F1 teams right now will have very few academic qualifications and may even struggle to use a computer. Does that surprise you? It should encourage you. You get a full spectrum from the mathematical genius to the practical hands-on fixers and teams need both, and all the people in between. The only question is where would you fit in?

Modern F1 teams are now much larger and employ many more people than they did 20 or even 10 years ago. Job roles and functions are more diverse and varied than ever. The days of everyone in the team being a mechanic or a driver are long gone.

Each F1 team employs somewhere between 200 and 1000 people depending on the budget that they have. When you include the engine design and development the headcount may be closer to 1500 for certain teams like Mercedes and Ferrari. That number may sound a lot just to allow two drivers to go motor racing but it is a measure of the complexity of the way the teams work and the different functions that they perform.

The F1 team therefore is much bigger than the group of people you see in the garage on television at the races. Every team is a working company which designs, manufactures and finances its own racing activities and the racing team is just the visible tip of that iceberg. Unlike many lower formula race outfits, F1 teams are actually small or medium sized engineering firms which design and manufacture high technology racing cars. Racing the cars is merely the end product of the vast research and development that goes on in the background and back at base.

As we have already seen, F1 teams are not just a racing outfit but they are working businesses which get involved in all of the day to day activities that any normal company requires. It just so happens that they manufacture racing cars as opposed to computers or cardboard boxes.

Detailed team structure is confidential and varies from team to team. I am not able to go into too much detail for those reasons. To give you an idea of how a typical team operates however I am going to create a fictional outfit called Ladbrooke F1. To show you how that team operates, I am going to split it up into 5 different functions and describe the sort of people who work in those areas and what they do. For Ladbrooke F1, those divisions are as follows:

- Design & Engineering
- Manufacturing & Assembly
- Marketing & PR
- Business Functions
- The Race team

To set the scene, Ladbrooke F1 is a team which designs and manufactures its own car but has an engine deal with a manufacturer. It is a successful outfit which has several strong commercial backers and invests much of its revenue in research and development looking to move itself up the grid. Although fictional (one day perhaps...), it should represent most of the teams on the current grid in some way or another. The largest section in most teams is normally the design & engineering group so let's start there as we work our way through the organisation as a whole.

Ladbrooke F1 - Design & Engineering

Whilst any racing team's prime function is to race, in Formula 1 your competitiveness is dependent on how good the design of your car is compared to the opposition. Even with the best drivers, a poorly designed car will not be able to compete with its faster and better engineered rivals. This is a basic truth. The engineering division of Ladbrooke F1 is organised to get the best out of its staff and is split into 3 general areas.

1) Aerodynamics

Aerodynamics has dominated Formula 1 for decades and Ladbrooke F1 puts more than half of its total engineering resource, including staff, into its aero programme. It has its own wind tunnel which is run and maintained by a team of technicians, ensuring that the fans, moving floor and delicate instrumentation provide accurate and reliable data for the aerodynamicists to examine.

Like all teams, Ladbrooke F1 uses a 50% or 60% scale model car rather than a real chassis for aerodynamic testing as it is generally cheaper, easier to modify and allows extra sensors and instrumentation to be incorporated inside the model to provide extra information. Recently the regulations have been changed to limit full size testing to the very minimum.

The model itself is a complicated machine more closely resembling a mobile laboratory than a car and so Ladbrooke F1 has a dedicated team of designers and technicians whose sole job is to create and maintain this critical piece of equipment and ensure it replicates the shape of the real car (or how it will look in the future) as closely as possible.

The aerodynamicists themselves study and compare track data from the real car, the windtunnel model and from computational fluid dynamics (CFD) to determine what shapes, wings and ideas produce the most downforce and least drag. They then use that knowledge to create further ideas to test and so the creative loop goes on. Gradually this process improves the car's performance over the course of a season and from year to year. The rate at which the team can make these improvements generally dictates its competitiveness on the grid and so Ladbrooke F1 places great emphasis on finding the best people it can to help in this area. This includes not only intelligent and knowledgeable aerodynamicists but also a dedicated team beneath them who bring those ideas to life.

Job Role	Description	Degree Required
Aerodynamicist	Creates aerodynamic shapes for the car and analyses data	Yes
CFD Engineer	Models fluid / airflow behaviour in simulation	Yes
Model Designer	Translates aerodynamicist's design into a working windtunnel model	Optional
Windtunnel Technician	Runs and maintains the windtunnel and its systems	No

2) Mechanical Design

This group of Ladbrooke F1 employees are responsible for the design of the real or full size car as it is generally known, packaging a working car into the aerodynamic shape passed to them by the aerodynamicists. Their work is done almost entirely on the Ladbrooke F1 3D computer aided design system (CAD) where a digital mock-up of the car can be built component by component to check that everything fits and works as it should before it is made. Their responsibilities include the suspension, steering, brakes and gearbox as well as the fuel and cooling systems to support the engine installation. Ladbrooke F1's specialist team of composites designers will then create the carbon fibre chassis, gearbox casing, crash structures and carbon bodywork that shrouds the inner workings of the car in its aerodynamic outer shape.

The full-size designer must ensure that his/her parts are just strong enough to survive the stresses and strains of racing yet lightweight enough to provide maximum performance and the lowest centre of gravity for the car. They will use exotic materials and a finite element analysis (FEA) package to help them achieve this, often with support from a dedicated FEA analyst. Together they strive to optimise each and every part of the car and create the smallest and lightest car on the grid.

Job Role	Description	Degree Required?
Mechanical Designer	Designs all of the metallic working parts of the car	Preferred
FEA engineer	Analyses and optimises each structural part for strength and weight	Yes
Composite Designer	Designs the carbon structures and bodywork plus the tooling to make it	Optional

3) Vehicle Dynamics and Performance

On track, Ladbrooke F1's car is a living, breathing machine which reacts to every corner, bump and kerb and driver input which is thrown at it. Understanding that behaviour and deciding how it can be improved is the job of the vehicle dynamicists.

The way that a Formula 1 car uses its tyres, reacts to downforce and rides uneven surfaces is an extremely complex discipline. Finding the ideal setup for the car is a series of compromises and trade-offs which constantly evolve circuit to circuit and as the design of the car is improved over the season. During race weekends, vehicle dynamicists back at base will pour over data coming from the car's on-board telemetry system to see how the ride heights, roll angles and balance of grip is changing through each and every corner. They can then advise the race team on what setup changes to make to improve performance and make the most of the car for the race.

Behind the scenes, they will also be refining computer simulations of their car's behaviour so that they can assess setup changes ahead of time and make recommendations to the design team for next year. This can be in the form of entirely computer based programs or using "driver in the loop" simulators where test or race drivers sit in a mock-up chassis and "drive" the car through large screens and a motion platform.

It is in this group where car performance evolves and many technical innovations are conceived. At Ladbrooke F1, this is the group where some of the most academically accomplished team members will work and PhD's are commonplace.

Job Role	Description	Degree Required?
Vehicle Dynamicist	Analyses and models car behaviour on track	Yes
Simulator Engineer	Works with test or dedicated simulator driver to analyse car setup	Yes
Tyre modeller	Develops detailed mathematical model of tyre behaviour	Yes

Ladbrooke F1 - Manufacturing & Assembly

As we have already seen although the Ladbrooke F1 team exists purely to race, the majority of the people employed by team are required in order to allow it to manufacture and develop the Ladbrooke F1 cars. Whilst the engineering boffins have free licence to dream up complex and sophisticated systems and designs for the car, the wider team also has to manufacture the various component parts and assemble them into a working and reliable machine. This is where technology again plays a major role but you may be surprised to hear that hands on skill is still essential in the production of the car. Formula 1 cars are low volume and constantly evolving prototypes and share little in common with the mass produced, production line style assembly of their road cars cousins. A huge amount of the car is made and assembled by hand and requires a great deal of skill and understanding to get right.

The knowledge and experience of Ladbrooke F1's shop floor and production staff is key to the success of our team and their contribution is as highly valued a commodity as the degree qualified designers who they work with.

1) Manufacturing

Ladbrooke F1 has extensive machining, composites and rapid prototyping facilities that allow it to make the vast majority of the car's component parts itself and to its own exacting standards. A substantial machine shop contains computer numerical controlled (CNC) lathes and milling machines which can produce a vast array of precision components from aerospace quality materials such as aluminium, titanium and magnesium. Skilled machinists program and run these devices 24 hours a day to keep up with the pace that new parts are released by the design team.

The composites group produce all kinds of components in carbon fibre from simple lightweight brackets, wings and bodywork to the complete chassis of the car. This work is hugely labour intensive with each ply of carbon having to be laminated by hand prior to curing in the autoclave (essentially a large oven) and then much of the final finishing of the parts being done by manual cutting and grinding. Composites work is a true craft and requires great skill and care to ensure quality and consistency.

Rapid prototyping (or 3D printing) has been in Formula 1 for decades and has been heavily utilised in production of windtunnel models where strength is less important but fast turnaround is a critical advantage. Ladbrooke F1 has a dedicated area in its production facility where several machines run 24 hours a day growing new parts for windtunnel testing. The limited properties of the materials compared to carbon or metallic parts have meant that it has been slow to make its way onto the car itself but the technology is used in some areas. This is likely to increase in the future as newer materials are developed which have properties better suited to lightweight structural applications.

Job Role	Description	Degree Required?
Manufacturing Engineer	Selects methods and technologies required to turn designs into high quality real parts	Optional
Machinist	Controls either manual or CNC machine to produce metallic parts	No
Fabricator	Forms and joins metallic parts like exhausts and radiator cores	No
Composite Laminator	Laminates carbon fibres over moulds to produce components	No
Composite Trimmer	Trims and finishes bodywork to get precision aerodynamic fit	No
3D printer operator	Sets up and responsible for 3D printer production	No
Quality Inspector	Measures and checks finished parts for quality and defects	No

2) Assembly

Ladbrooke F1's cars are normally put together at the circuit prior to each race and can often be rebuilt overnight when necessary, after accident damage or reliability issues. This is the job of the race team mechanics that we will come across later in this chapter.

It often impresses newcomers to the sport just how quickly a crashed or damaged car can be fixed and rebuilt, re-appearing on television for the following practice or qualifying session as if nothing had happened. Part of this is the skill and dedication of the mechanics themselves but it is also because major parts of the car are pre-built at the factory by sub-assembly technicians ready to be swapped or fitted to a bare chassis.

Each gearbox for example will arrive at the circuit assembled with ratios, pumps and hydraulics ready to be fitted to the engine. Each box will however also have a full set of rear suspension, wishbones, springs, dampers, uprights, brake discs and cooling ducts and not only that but it will come pre-fitted with its rear wing assembly and drag reduction system(DRS). It is a complete rear end of the car and can literally be bolted up, bled and fired up ready to go out on track.

Much of this pre-assembly is done back at the factory by specialist technicians who take each component part and build up larger assemblies, check them for function and legality and load them onto the trucks ready to go the race track. These same technicians will strip and service each sub-assembly between races, changing bearings, seals and fasteners, cleaning the components parts and checking them for defects and cracks before rebuilding.

Precision parts such as hydraulics, pumps and engines are never worked on at the circuit as they often require clean room conditions to ensure that there is no environmental contamination in the system that could cause a failure and specialist tools to set clearances. This kind of work is critical behind the scenes but rarely seen on television. It is the job of highly skilled individuals who often have years of experience in their field, many having been race mechanics themselves in previous seasons.

Job Role	Description	Degree Required?
Gearbox Technician	Assembles and sets up gearbox assemblies, clusters and differentials	No
Sub-assembly Technician	Builds complex assemblies such as uprights and suspension parts	No
Hydraulics Technician	Builds precision assemblies such as pumps, power steering & DRS	No
NDT technician	Uses non-destructive testing techniques to check for faults and defects	No

Ladbrooke F1 - Marketing & PR

Racing teams exist to race. Almost every person working in F1 does so because they enjoy the challenge of competition and the thrill of speed. Racing is the reason that Formula 1 continues to spread its popularity and why fans are willing to pay to come and watch it.

Formula 1 however is not purely sport, it's an entertainment business. It's also extremely expensive. In football, you can play just with a ball and a group of friends in the back yard. Tennis rackets might be expensive but not beyond the reach of the vast majority and even golf club membership is not totally prohibitive if you enjoy it sufficiently.

Motor racing however is different. The cost of a year's racing in the junior formulas can run to several hundred thousand dollars and is beyond the means of all but the super-rich. Sponsorship and commercial backing is an integral part of almost all racing and in particular Formula 1. If you believe that an F1 team's competitiveness is dictated to by its budget then marketing is potentially the most important function within the whole team.

Ladbrooke F1 is a privately owned team and so does not have a parent company filling its bank account each month. It relies on its sponsors and commercial agreements to generate the budget that it needs to go racing. The marketing team has courted and retained several major backers, including a title sponsor who's branding form the team image and colour scheme both at the circuit and at the factory. Formula 1 is televised and featured in online and print media across the world and the marketing department are focused on leveraging that exposure and the image that it has created to provide value for money advertising and branding benefits for all of its commercial partners.

Partnerships are managed by account managers who build close relationships with key people at the partnering company and discuss arrangements, branding or events which can be of mutual benefit to both parties. It's typically their job to ensure that each relationship is maximised and that all opportunities are looked at and exploited. This provides maximum return and ensures that partnerships are maintained over as long a term as possible.

New sponsors and partners are always being courted and it is not unheard of for sponsorships to be started after several years of discussion and negotiation. This new business will be sought by senior marketing people and requires persistence and optimism as it can be a frustratingly slow business even for very successful teams.

Marketing is much more sophisticated than just a sticker on the car these days and teams will aim to involve their partners in the team as much as possible, organising events at the factory and races where corporate hospitality is very comprehensive. Imagine if your business could organise meetings with potential clients on the Ferrari yacht at Monaco, it's sure to impress. This type of positive association is part of what sponsorship gets you and can be effective in all sorts of ways. Event managers are responsible for putting on the parties, transport and entertainment that make partners and their clients feel like they are part of the action and can often bring F1 to the sponsor's premises through show cars and driver appearances. It's all part of the service and creating new and inventive ways of improving that service is a key part of the marketing department's role.

Media interest in Formula 1 is very high and so relations with the press are very important. Race results, driver quotes and sponsorship announcements are all made through press releases and conferences where relevant media are invited to hear from the team. The opinion of journalists often strongly reflects on the image of the team and so good media relations are nearly as important as partner relationships. Teams will often entertain journalists and provide hospitality to ensure that their team is projected to the world in a positive light, further strengthening its commercial bargaining position.

Social and other digital media are fast growing areas of communication for F1 teams and they are finding ways to leverage their followings to increase brand awareness and effectiveness. Most teams now have dedicated digital media people to create and run their campaigns and also to monitor and reply to user responses. Controversies and racing incidents can be managed or promoted to benefit the team image and the power of these new channels is growing season by season. The use of these new technologies is still in its relative infancy in Formula 1 and is likely to grow over the next few years so opportunities for energetic and experienced individuals in the area are likely to increase also.

Job Role	Description	Degree Required?
Event organiser	Plans and organises sponsor events and entertains clients	No
Account Manager	Works with sponsors to ensure best value and benefit for all parties	Preferred
Marketing Manager	Seeks new partners and sponsor and guides overall marketing strategy	Preferred
Graphics Designer	Designs team branding including clothing and car livery	No
Social Media Manager	Coordinates and runs social media campaigns	No

Ladbrooke F1 - Business Functions

Formula 1 is an extraordinary business is many ways but it is easy to lose sight of the fact that Ladbrooke F1 is just an ordinary company the same as any other. As such it needs all of the same functions and services that other small or medium sized businesses require in order for it to function from day to day. F1 teams have accountants, receptionists, van drivers, IT support, cleaning services, catering, site maintenance and site security in the same way as most other non-racing companies. This fact allows completely non-technical people or those without any prior racing experience to work in F1. In many cases these general roles provide an access point from which you can get further involved in the racing business.

Purchasing and logistics is a critical area of Formula 1 and a business function where individuals can make a vast difference to the performance of a team. Buyers who can develop close relationships with suppliers can negotiate faster lead times and improve the development rate of new aerodynamic parts or mechanical upgrades. Getting parts and people to and from racing circuits is a constant and fast moving activity in F1 and Ladbrooke F1 relies heavily on its transport people to be organised and responsive to meet the needs of the racing season. It's not uncommon for van drivers to go straight from suppliers to the airport to meet team managers who are hand carrying critical parts to the other side of the world just in time to make the build for first practice. Organising that and ensuring that everyone knows what is happening takes a dedicated individual and good people in this part of the business are worth their weight in gold.

In many of these roles there is nothing written in the job description that is racing specific and so they are open to anyone outside of the racing business with suitable qualifications or experience. What will be evident however is that F1 teams will still be looking for that same can do attitude and team spirit that it demands from all of its staff whether technical or not. Success is an attitude that runs from top to bottom and any of an F1 team's staff may be called upon to help out when the need arises. I have seen an 18 year old maintenance apprentice travel to Melbourne for the weekend to deliver last minute aerodynamic upgrades to the race team and watch the Grand Prix from a prime pit lane seat. Day to day operation it may be, but this is still an extraordinary business.

The general nature of these roles makes them open to a wider audience but also makes them slightly harder to target as an aspiring F1 worker. Many vacancies will only be advertised locally or in role specific publications rather than in the motorsport press. If you can find those openings then competition for them might be lower than for the headline grabbing race team jobs. A small start perhaps but these roles can often be the start point of a motorsport orientated career if you can grab the bull by the horns and demonstrate that you have what it takes to win.

Job Role	Description	Degree Required?
Technical Buyer	Sources components from suppliers to meet production demand	No
Software Engineer	Writes and maintains bespoke software for internal use	Yes
Logistics Coordinator	Arranges transport of people & parts to/from circuits	No
Accountant	Handles payments and invoices from sponsors and suppliers	Preferred
IT support	Internal and trackside IT support to keep computer system running	Optional
Receptionist	Meets and greets drivers, sponsors, press and other factory visitors	No

Ladbrooke F1 - The Race Team

No matter what high technology and fast moving business functions occur at the factory, the heart of any Formula 1 team is its race team. Ladbrooke F1 is no exception and this is where its race cars are brought to life and the hard work and ideas of every employee in the team are put to the test. This is the essence of Formula 1.

Ladbrooke F1's race team is a dedicated part of the company which includes mechanics, race engineers, 'truckies' and a scattering of support staff who may either be full time with the crew or factory based staff that travel to a handful of races each year on a rota type basis. The race team has to be near self sufficient, capable of assembling and running the cars but also building its own garage, installing IT equipment, communications, feeding itself and entertaining guests. It is a massive operation which moves from race to race and continent to continent sometimes just a week apart. Being on the race team is hard work.

With the majority of races still being in and around Europe, the most common mode of transport for the race team equipment is by truck. Having helped pack up the equipment, race cars and spares back at the factory, the truckies are normally the first to arrive at the circuit to unload and setup the garage and working areas for the team. Once done, the truckies will typically have a secondary role such as sorting tyre sets, ensuring each has appropriate blankets and to check the function of pit stop equipment, fuel and lubricants. On race day it's quite common for one or more of the truck drivers to be involved in the pit stops, being either a jack man or tyre changer depending on their skills and physique.

The race team mechanics will generally fly to races, arriving on the Wednesday before the race to finish the car build and prepare them for the event. For a customer team like Ladbrooke F1, engines will often to shipped to the races directly from the manufacturer and so these will need to be fitted, followed by the gearboxes, oil, water and hydraulic lines before the floors, bodywork and final checks can be made and carried out prior to scrutineering and FIA legality checks. This activity is coordinated by the chief mechanic who liaises between the engineering team and the number 1 mechanics for each car as to what work needs to be done.

The engine will be then fired up for the first time and a series of checks performed on the gearshift, drag reduction system and brake by wire. A problem at this point will mean a lengthy tear down and rebuild of the car that can go on long into the night and into Thursday. The final job is to setup the car according to the race engineer's required weight distribution, ride heights, cambers and toes ready for the first runs in practice the following morning.

The mechanics will also have a Sunday role as the pit crew and will take their places as gun men, jack operators and tyre handlers. This requires extensive practice both at the factory and at the race track. The crew are often rotated and any member of the team who does not have another critical role to play during the race can take part if their physique and skills are suitable. This could include the truckies, engine kitters or hydraulics technicians. Traditionally the chief mechanic would operate the stop/go lollipop to release the driver but this role is becoming increasingly redundant as more teams move to an automated traffic light system.

Ladbrooke F1's race engineering team is normally the last to arrive having stayed longer at the factory to work with vehicle dynamics on set ups, strategy predictions and run plans for the coming event. Race meetings are now very structured as the on-track time is quite limited and typically a free practice session is planned down to the nearest minute as to when the car will go out, what tyres will be fitted and how many laps are to be run. Very few decisions are left to chance as time lost deliberating what to do next is wasted track time and so a full programme of aerodynamic tests, tyre comparisons and setup changes is planned in advance. The plan is documented right down to the number of practice starts, burnouts, where to stop the car in the pit lane, radio checks at each corner of the circuit, when to use DRS, the speed of the outlaps, tyre pressures and fuel loads on each run.

The race engineer is responsible for running a car at the race track and is the central point of contact between the driver and the rest of the team. A close working relationship here is critical and it is important for the race engineer to shelter the driver from all of the distraction and activity that goes on in the background. He/she must be skilled in getting the right feedback back from the driver and also ensuring that the driver knows what settings to use and when to get the correct information back to the engineers in the garage and at the factory. Coordination and communication is a key skill as well as the ability to understand the car's behaviour and fine tune it to get the most out of it.

The race engineer is closely supported by the data engineers who monitor the telemetry screens checking that the car is behaving as expected or assessing what adjustments are required to make it perform better. If the driver complains that the car is unstable under braking for example, the data engineer should be able to confirm that from the telemetry and often tell the race engineer why. It may be due to brake temperatures being out of their optimum window, the ride heights being wrong or the driver downshifting too late and so this information is then used to make adjustments to the setup or fed back to the driver so that they can make improvements.

Detailed driver controls such as clutch, gearbox, differential, brake balance, throttle map and other engine functions are maintained by the control engineers who ensure that these electronically controlled functions are optimised and setup exactly as the driver wishes. The complexity of a modern F1 steering wheel is well documented and the control engineers are responsible for assigning functions, displays and messages to the various switches and buttons available to the driver so that he can maximise the car's performance at various stages of the lap and the race itself.

The other positions on the pitwall will be filled by the chief race engineer, strategists and team managers. The chief race engineer oversees the whole of the track engineering operation and will make any decisive calls that need to be made in the interests of the team. The strategist's role is clear during races but they will also be well occupied during practice analysing competitor performance, tyre degradation and overtaking potential. Their role is to supply as much data and information to race engineers as they can to help them maximise the potential of the car during the race.

The team manager oversees the whole of the track operation from engineering to the truckies and is responsible for representing the team to the FIA via radio communication and in the steward's office should any driver be involved in a contentious issue. They will normally have many years of track experience to draw upon.

Job Role	Description	Degree Required?
Control Engineer	Responsible for optimising gearbox, brake by wire & start performance	Yes
Data Engineer	Analyses detailed car data and provides support to Race Engineer	Yes
Race Engineer	Responsible for car performance and communicating with driver	Preferred
Chief Engineer	Oversees track engineering and communication across cars	Yes
Strategist	Analyses and generates data to aid decision making during races	Yes
Team Manager	Responsible for team operation at track and FIA communication	No
Truckie	Transports equipment to track, garage setup and pitstop role	No

Number 2 Mechanic	Assembly of car sub-section such as front or rear suspension plus takes a role in pitstops	No
Number 1 Mechanic	Senior mechanic on one car and may take a pitstop role	No
Chief Mechanic	Responsible for all overseeing mechanics & typically operates lollipop during pitstops	No

The list above is by no means exhaustive but I hope that it gives you some idea of the diversity of roles within a typical F1 team and the differences in day to day responsibility. Most of the roles described could be sub-divided further and there is plenty of variety in jobs roles and structure team to team but this list should be a good start.

Whilst it is important to have a clear idea of what you want to do it is not necessary to pick just a single role at this very moment and commit to it. There is so much crossover and similarity between many of the roles within a particular division that you can reconsider as you get closer to your goal and quite often fate plays a part in where you might end up. Until you do the role for real you will never really know what suits you but to start with a target in mind gives you a goal to channel your energy into.

The first 4 of the 5 team functions that I have described above broadly represent the different educational paths and choices that you might have to make as you prepare yourself for work in motorsport. These broad choices, such as whether you want to be in marketing or in design are quite fundamental and will influence whether you go to university or what subject areas you choose to study.

Once established in your first job in racing it is only then that you begin to specialise into a very specific role within that chosen area depending on your opportunities, preferences and particular skills. After 3 to 5 years of work experience within the industry that you are likely to be focussing on one specific role and becoming a specialist in that narrow area. Some crossover between the broader functions is always possible of course (engineering to marketing for example) but might involve returning to education or learning a new trade or set of skills. It is much better to consider your options now and be sure that you have chosen the right area for you. Deciding at an early stage between these broader functions and whether you want or need to take degree is probably as detailed as you need to get at this stage.

As we have seen, the race team is something of a specialist case as it involves individuals from a broad snapshot of the company as a whole and is open to most individuals in some capacity. We will discuss educational choices and routes into Formula 1 in more detail in Parts 4 and 5.

2 What job can I do in F1?

The diversity of roles and skills within a modern F1 team make a career in Formula 1 a realistic target for many people from a range of backgrounds. Given a free choice I am sure that many of you would choose to be the driver for obvious reasons but being realistic and considering your own strengths and weaknesses as well as your interests and desires will help you focus and target a role which gives you the greatest chance of success. Having a focused goal in mind is key to maintaining motivation and will tell any potential team that you have done your research and understand what the team may expect of you. Too many people stop at simply wanting a job in F1 without considering exactly *which* job they are best suited for and lose their way as a result.

I've worked in motorsport and Formula 1 for many, many years now. Over those years, I have accumulated knowledge and experience which helps me do my job well (I hope) and contribute to the team's performance. I am well aware however that if I were to be asked to take the role of a race mechanic or composite trimmer for example I would be an embarrassment to the team and would likely be sacked in a matter of days. The knowledge that I have is in fact quite narrow and I am in awe of the skill and abilities of many other people within our team whose job I would have no hope of doing as quickly and as skilfully as they are able to do. Even working in the industry already does not mean that I can do any job in F1 that I like and realistically neither will you.

You may have decided (as I did) at an early age that working in motorsport was your career aim but to maximise your chances you need to recognise in more detail where your skills and interests lie and make the decisions that help you to develop those skills. The previous chapter described a typical team in Formula 1 and the job roles that make up the organisation. This chapter is about deciding which roles you see yourself doing and which you would be best suited to. This choice may affect which qualifications and work experience you should pursue and even how to approach a team for employment.

Formula 1 is quite unique in motorsport in that it is as much, if not more, about the design of the cars as it is about the drivers and the racing. In most forms of motor racing, including the so called lower formulas, team owners or drivers will simply buy a car from a competitor or direct from the manufacturer and run it at a race meeting. They will need to maintain it and may spend some time modifying or tuning it with alternative parts that they have bought or adapted from other vehicles but in essence they are a race team and not a racing car manufacturer.

Race series such as Formula Ford, F3, GP3 and GP2 all fall into this category. The cars are essentially all the same, of a single make, with the competitiveness of a team largely decided by the way it prepares and sets up its car and the skill of its driver. The size of the team may vary from 1 or 2 individuals in Formula Ford to 10-15 for a multicar GP2 team. In general terms however they are all very small and there is no need for the design and manufacturing functions that we require in Formula 1. People often talk of working your way up the racing ladder in the same way as the drivers do but this is only relevant for trackside jobs in F1 which have similarities to those you find in those same lower formulas. In reality this is only a very small proportion of all the jobs in Formula 1 and so for the majority of roles, working in a lower formula is not necessarily the best preparation.

It's a common mistake to think that this racing ladder for drivers is the only way into Formula 1 for other people but the wider motorsport industry is in fact much, much larger than many expect and as such it offers many different ladders and ways of gaining experience prior to working in F1. All racing experience is valuable but it's perfectly possible to work in motorsport without ever going to a race meeting or holding a wrench or spanner.

Supplier companies to motorsport teams and manufacturers of racing cars employ a great number of people in the industry, probably more than the race teams themselves and they require the same broad spectrum of skills and qualifications that a Formula 1 team may need. The range of job opportunities and experiences is much more diverse in the motorsport supplier sector than it is in small racing ladder teams and it's important to separate the scope of the job roles available to you from purely those within the function of a race team.

As we touched on in the previous chapter, it is not necessary to commit to a job role at this stage or even to a career path to get you there. Having said that however, knowledge of the industry and the types of roles that it requires will help you to focus and hone your skills in the right manner. Making some early choices and asking yourself some fundamental questions is key before starting out and so I would recommend thinking about the types of activities you enjoy and those you feel you are good at. Comparing those activities against the job roles we described in the previous chapter will help you find your niche where you might fit within F1. For example, if you enjoy fixing things, taking things apart and getting your hands dirty then you could be well suited to a mechanic's role or in sub-assembly. If you enjoy numbers and working out why and how things work or consider yourself a bit of a technology geek then you might want to consider being a design engineer or aerodynamicist. If you enjoy classroom learning and study then you may enjoy taking degree course at university but it isn't for everyone and certainly isn't necessary for every job in Formula 1.

There are some good bits of advice out there but one of the best accounts I have heard is from Mark Priestly who was a mechanic at McLaren for many, many years. He stayed on at school but soon found he had a longing to get out to work and made the brave move to quit his A-levels and start as a junior mechanic. He has had a fantastically varied and successful career which has seen him involved in many Grand Prix wins. You can read his account here:

http://jobinf1.com/2015/03/15/how-to-become-an-f1-mechanic-by-f1-elvis/

Asking yourself these fundamental questions will help you focus on what it is you want from your career and what route you are prepared to take to get to that goal. It's no good setting your sights on being an aerodynamicist if you don't wish to study for example because you will need a degree for this job. In this case, you will need to study hard to understand the complex theories involved and these are not typically ideas that can be picked up on the job. Likewise, if you don't like physical work or building machines you are unlikely to enjoy being a trackside mechanic. Traditionally these kinds of differences were separated as being either blue collar or white collar roles, or in other words shop floor versus office jobs. I personally believe that these divisions are outdated, particularly in Formula 1 but as a starting point it may be useful to consider which category you might see yourself as. Try and imagine what your day will be like, where you will be working and what type of people you will be working with and for. Broad choices at this stage will help you prepare yourself for the more detailed decisions that you may need to make over the next few years.

In recruitment, I often hear potential candidates use the phrase "give me a job" but I cringe each time I hear that. If only life was that easy. The plain truth is that nobody is going to *give* you a job in F1 or in any other walk of life for that matter, you need to earn it by offering something in return. Begging is not likely to get you very far and it's important to understand that being successful in getting work in Formula 1 is not a case of pleading harder than the next guy or girl. Formula 1 is far from being charitable.

Instead, it's important to consider any job as a way of solving a need for the employer. When a team or any other employer tries to recruit, they have a need or a shortage of skills and this is a problem which they need to solve. The trick to getting that job is to fulfil that need by supplying the skills or experience that the team needs to solve that problem. Knowing what those needs are is the reason it is so important to understand the industry and what the job roles are within an F1 team. Once you understand what the employer needs from you, you will be much better placed to gain those skills and offer them in your applications. You may not have worked at an F1 team before but you can still solve its needs by supplying appropriate and similar skills gained elsewhere in racing or in other applicable industries. The team is not just *giving* jobs away, it needs skills and experience from you as part of the deal so you need to realise what those requirements are likely to be well before you apply.

Once you start to think about recruitment as a two-way exchange you will be more effective and are far more likely to take responsibility for your own career development. So many young people that I meet rely on school to prepare them for the world of work and believe that simply choosing a particular course or subject at school that the education system will lead them into their chosen job role. Don't rely on this, it won't be enough. Don't get me wrong, it is vital to study and good grades will always looked upon favourably but your character and abilities are far wider ranging that a set of exam results. Developing yourself is also vital and F1 teams really value the skills and character traits that extracurricular activities bring out in you. A candidate who can demonstrate initiative, diversity and enthusiasm, backed up by strong school or college results is exactly what the teams are looking for. There are many, many ways that you can build experience and character whilst you study so don't think that you can only get that by working in racing.

F1 teams need employees who think for themselves, make things happen and push the team forward. Success comes from pushing the boundaries and exploring things that have never been done before. The most successful teams are full of these self-driven and inventive people who make their own opportunities.

When we recruit we want to hear from the brightest and most promising people. We want to hear from people who can show us how motivated they are, demonstrate that they have pushed themselves and show that they can be different from the crowd. This does not simply mean those people who have the best grades from school.

If you come to us having relied only on your school to prepare you, with a CV which has only a list of subjects and exam grades on it then I am afraid you are not likely to get hired. We get so many of these applications and they can look quite empty and hard to distinguish from one another. Nothing in your application tells me whether you will be someone who pushes forward, who can take responsibility and improve something or make the best of a difficult situation. I won't be able to tell whether I can rely on you and will worry that you will need to be told what to do and how to do it. You may have done well at school but you need a different set of skills to be successful at work and I can't take a risk on you without seeing more evidence that you can think on your feet and help my team succeed.

Understanding my needs and solving them through your skills and experience is the two- way exchange of every job. Learning about the world of motorsport is how you will come to understand what we want from you and how you will be able to demonstrate it. If you arrive at my door will both a good education and the ability to show that you have been out and experienced real world motorsport (or something equivalent) and tried to get involved then our door will be wide open to you. You will be solving a need and will have earned a job in Formula 1.

One of the unique aspects of motorsport compared to other industries is the fact that so many people race or help out with racing as their hobby, not just as their career. This opens up a wealth of opportunity to get out there and experience something very similar to a professional role before you get a real job in the industry. The benefits of this are several but one of the key advantages is when you are still deciding what job role it is that you will be most suited to. Hobby level motorsport gives you the chance to try out various aspects of the job and see first hand what they might involve. Don't get me wrong, unless you are very fortunate then it's unlikely that you will be doing voluntary work at a Formula 1 team whilst you are still school but that isn't the point. Just being at a race track or helping to prepare a real racing car gives you a fantastic insight into what working in Formula 1 is like because even club level racing or karting share so many parallels with F1. Being involved in motorsport helps you understand the industry and try out various roles long before you take paid employment.

Fixing a 1970's Mini rally car may seem like a world away from preparing one of today's ultra-sophisticated F1 hybrid cars but in actual fact the skills required and content of the job are fundamentally the same. If you can demonstrate that you are competent and experienced at preparing the old rally car then the transition across to the Formula 1 will be relatively straight forward. If you have never held a spanner or changed a spark plug before then you might find Formula 1 a bit too much of a steep learning curve. These are small steps perhaps but the more time you spend around motorsport and learning about what goes on in that environment the clearer your mind will be about what it is you want to do and what that job involves. All racing is fundamentally the same, it just takes place on a different scale and budget. Confidence will come from the lower level experiences you get and that can only motivate you more to push for your ultimate goals at the pinnacle of the sport.

There are a vast number of different jobs that you can do in Formula 1 and there is nothing to stop you from doing whatever you choose. You may feel at this stage that you don't have the skills necessary to do any of the jobs we have talked about so far but there is only one way to go out and change that. The more you know about the job you want to do the more focussed you can be as you chase the dream of doing it. Learning is key at this stage through both real life experience and through reading and studying. Knowledge is built up in small steps stage by stage but getting started is often the most difficult part. Once you know and understand what you want then going after it and achieving it becomes a great deal easier. That stage is the subject of the next few chapters of this book.

3 What are winners made of and do I have the right stuff?

Whilst Formula 1 has its fair share of boffins, geniuses and degree qualified inventors, the difference between winning and losing is often nothing to do with exam grades and qualifications. When it comes to pressure situations and a competitive environment your attitude and mindset are often more important than what you achieved at school. Being able to demonstrate that you have these kinds of character attributes is critical when it comes to getting a job in F1.

As we already know, F1 is a unique business especially when you consider that such a small team of people can design, manufacture, build, transport and race a high technology car at race tracks all over the world. Something special must allow that small group of people to achieve all that in such a short space of time and it has little to do with good management, company systems or corporate mission statements. The individual resolve, attitude and will power of the F1 team's employees is what allows it to excel against the odds and then as a group produce what is necessary go racing and to be competitive. They say that people are a company's most valuable asset and that is never more true than in Formula 1. F1 people set themselves apart by being highly self motivated, dedicated and never accepting defeat.

In this chapter I hope to convey how important attitude can be and provide real world examples of how work ethic and commitment can make as big a difference to a team's success as qualifications or knowledge. I'll try and put you into the shoes of the team managers and senior engineers and to show you how critical it is for them to be able to rely upon their team members. If you want to work in F1 it is as important to demonstrate that you share this F1 attitude and work ethic as it is to show that you have the right skills and qualifications. There are no exams or certificates which can qualify you for this so your achievements and extracurricular activities will be the way in which you demonstrate that you have what it takes.

The dreaded phrase "2 years minimum experience in Formula 1 or other high level motorsport" accompanies almost all job adverts that you see in the motorsport press or on F1 team's websites. If every advert and job role carries this requirement it may seem impossible for newcomer to break the cycle and get a job in Formula 1. If no-one will allow you to prove yourself how will you ever gain that minimum experience? This conundrum reinforces the belief that F1 is a closed and insular business that is only open to those people who know somebody on the inside. I can tell you that this isn't the case but many of you will not believe me, at least not yet.

Let me explain to you a little more about why that phrase is so often tagged onto the end of the advert for your dream job in Formula 1. It is not necessarily to be taken at face value. Experience in motorsport counts for a lot, I won't try to convince you otherwise but the stipulation for motorsport experience in job advertisements is not just about experience alone. It is more commonly used as a way to filter out people who are not suited to, or not committed to the demands that a motorsport job places on them. As I mentioned earlier on in this chapter, there are no examinations or qualifications that tell you about a person's attitude and commitment and as a result an employer such as a Formula 1 team is at great risk when recruiting. They may be able to find people who have PhD's and the highest exam grades in their field but if those same people do not have a Formula 1 mindset then they will not be the right people for the team. The team wants to avoid making the wrong choices.

When a recruiter from a Formula 1 team sees an application with previous motorsport experience in it they will instantly know that that person is likely to understand the commitment required by F1. That is the first step. The very fact that that same person is applying for a further job in the industry suggests that they are prepared to continue at that level and are more likely to have the sort of attitude that the team is looking for. There is no guarantee that this person is good of course but it reduces that risk considerably. Many people will tell you that they are committed, but until they have worked in the kind of environment that Formula 1 creates, they are unlikely to know it themselves. Many people decide that Formula 1 is not for them once they get the chance to experience it.

It is not uncommon for newcomers to the sport to leave after a year (or less in some cases) and to go and get a more ordinary job in a different industry. This is perfectly understandable but it means that it leaves the team with a hole which takes time to fill. Worse still, they may not leave at all but coast along and fail to deliver at a critical moment, letting the team down and all those they work with. Either way it has been a costly and poor recruitment and if this happens too often it will harm the team's competitiveness. Filtering out these uncommitted individuals, no matter how smart they may be, is a critical part of the recruitment process.

This is why the teams are so afraid of giving you a chance. They don't know anything about you. The difficulty that you will have and much of the effort you need to make should be aimed at building up a record of commitment that you can use to convince an F1 team that you have the right mindset and are the type of person they need in their team. You don't need 2 years of motorsport experience to do this despite what the adverts say but you will need spend time and effort building up something which can impress the team.

All kinds of people work in Formula 1. Some have degrees and PhD s, others can't even add up or spell. It takes all sorts but one thing you will see in almost every Formula 1 employee is a racer's mindset. Trying to define the racer s mindset is difficult but it is fundamental to any discussion on working in F1. What sets Formula 1 and motorsport apart from normal industries is not the technology, or the money, or the glitz and glamour. What sets motor racing apart is the work ethic and the competitive motivation that runs through its employees. To get a job in F1 you need to understand what this mindset is and be able to convince your potential employer that you have the work ethic they are looking for. As we have said previously, it is not about the team giving you a job, you need to be ready to present yourself as a solution to the team's needs and not merely as a hopeful fan.

To demonstrate what I mean, imagine this scene. It is Saturday morning and the crew of Ladbrooke F1 are 40mins into FP3 (the final free practice session before qualifying begins). The live TV feed on the monitor cuts abruptly to show a cloud of dust and bits of carbon fibre bodywork scattered through a gravel trap. Even before the dust clears the team manager comes on the radio to confirm that your lead driver has crashed heavily into a tyre wall and the car looks to be badly damaged. Qualifying is less than 2 hours away and missing Q1 means that you'll start at the back of the grid (or not at all), a disaster for the championship. The car has got to be repaired and back out no matter what. It is your call to action.

It's a familiar story in racing and to the casual TV viewer the repaired car normally appears clean and polished for qualifying as if nothing had happened. It must be easy mustn't it? Wrong - it's far from easy. It is situations such as these when the Formula 1 mindset is most evident. What goes on inside those pit garages during times like these is truly, truly impressive teamwork and the ethic and drive of the individuals is the key to making it work.

The mechanics were probably up late last night building the very same car after numerous last minute setup and aero changes. They've been at the circuit since 7am and had too much to do to stop for breakfast. Their driver's latest mistake has just written off any chance of a lunch break and they are faced with a massive task to get that car rebuilt and turned around reliably for qualifying. They don't wait until they're told what to do, they are already up and getting the spare suspension kits, floor, front wing & nose ready and laying out the garage with the tools, garage jacks and kit they will need to repair the car. Two of the junior mechanics have already left the paddock in one of the hire cars and are travelling round the service road to get to the car to ensure that is loaded onto the truck quickly and carefully and to get an initial assessment of the damage so that they can call back to the pits. Minutes saved here might mean the difference between qualifying and not.

Even once the car is back, they can't afford to leave a nut loose or an electrical lead unconnected just because they are under pressure. They are more than likely furious with their driver but there is no use in complaining at this point because the job just needs doing. In any normal industry people would moan about being over worked and underpaid. In F1 the only thing on your mind should be the disaster that not making qualifying would mean for your championship chances. Even if your team is only expected to qualify at the back of the grid, you've still got to want to get the car back out and everyone is relying on you to make the difference. There is no hiding, you need to be the person that people can rely on to do your job whilst they get on with theirs. Even once the car is back out there will be the pressure of qualifying and the need to give your all to get the most out of it. The expectation is relentless.

This probably all sounds quite glamorous and exciting but cutting through the fantasy you should ask yourself if you would truly want to be a part of a world like this? For a one off weekend I think we would all jump at the chance, but quite often there is a big conflict between work and outside commitments. To want this life as your career you need to be driven and motivated to succeed through the conflict and enjoy racing for what it is. When your friends are off for the weekend and you cannot join them because of work commitments you need to be able to justify that as part of the choice you have made. You cannot take all the benefits of working in F1 without some of the strain and the demands it places on you. If you walk away when your effort is most needed then you may not last too long in this job.

Formula 1 attracts motivated, aspirational people who enjoy the challenge of competition. To be successful in this environment you must want to push yourself and to push others to a common goal. If you are competitive and driven to better yourself then you will be well suited to working in this sport. If you are the type of person who is never satisfied and always wants to improve then we want to hear from you. It's hard to know if you truly have what it takes before you do the job for real but by putting yourself into competitive and demanding situations then you put yourself to the test and develop those aspects of your personality. Racing awoke my own competitive spirit and gave my life real direction for the first time. Formula 1 might have still been a long way away at that point but getting involved in grass roots motorsport and learning to deal with the demands of competing convinced me that I could deal with it and that I wanted to do it. When faced with difficult situations later in my F1 career and the pressure of having to make decisions I recognised the feelings as being just the same as I had felt years earlier in karting and whilst helping in club racing. The stakes might be higher but the demands are just the same and I knew that I could handle it because of those early experiences. Grass root competition taught me almost everything I know about racing.

To learn if racing is for you and whether you have what it takes I suggest you put yourself to the test. Get out and get involved. If you struggle to find an opportunity to do that then great, it's a test of your resolve. How far are you prepared to go to find that experience? Keep looking and try harder. If you don't want to spend your weekends at the race track trying to make contacts then perhaps you have answered your own question and should stick to watching F1 on television. If your struggles only harden your resolve to make it and the frustration drives you to succeed then congratulations, you probably have what it takes. The path is never easy and straightforward and you should not expect it to be. The lessons you learn along the way will tell you whether this life is for you and whether you have what it takes.

The demands of racing cannot be taught through school books. As far as I know there are no qualifications or exams that show that you have the right attitude. In Formula 1 you should be motivated by the racing itself to give you the required level of commitment and then demonstrate that through the things that you have achieved. If you are a team owner or team manager you desperately need people of the right mindset and calibre in your racing team. When the pressure is on, either at the racetrack or at the factory, nobody cares how many PhD s or degrees you have as the people who make the difference are the people who are self motivated and determined to get the job done properly. Sometimes the job just needs doing and if you walk away at the critical moment then you will have let your team down.

The work that you do under pressure is the real measure of your ability. F1 people take pride in their work, do more than is asked of them, are never satisfied and strive to find ways to do it better. At school, you have a curriculum to follow and if you achieve that you will get a high grade. It serves a purpose, but it does not always encourage individual thinking or inventiveness. It does not prepare you for that late pre-qualifying crisis or another high pressure situation at the factory. Education is not just about school it is about life and that is why it is so important to seek extra-curricular experience alongside your formal qualifications.

The ability to demonstrate that you have gone out of your way to gain further experience and learnt from those experiences will be your qualifications in real life. It is not an easy thing to convince a potential employer of and you should take some considerable time developing this area of your resume. Given how much time we spend at school and how hard we study then outside activities are often neglected in comparison. The balance should be much more even and that is a core message of this book. I hope to demonstrate how you can achieve this balance.

These extracurricular activities will be the mechanism by which you show that you have the Formula 1 mindset and the attitude necessary to succeed in Formula 1. In an interview, it is very hard to talk about exams or the curriculum and so your outside activities will be the key things that you can discuss and that will make you stand out from the majority. These are the qualities that F1 teams need from you and are the skills that they will be looking for you to demonstrate to them. They will need to be convinced by you and what you have done with your life. They need to be convinced that you are someone who can be relied upon when they need you.

Striking out on your own, seeking your own experiences and making your own opportunities is what you need to think about to develop a Formula 1 mindset and I will be telling you exactly how you can do this later in Part 4.

4 What F1 wants from you - essential skills

As we have seen gradually over the previous chapters, success in Formula 1 can be as much about personal qualities as it is about academic or formal qualifications. If you want to be a success in Formula 1 you need to develop a balance of essential skills and crucially you need to be able to convey them through the experience and the initiative that you have shown to get you where you are today. There are no exams or qualifications that can prove that you have these qualities, you need to develop and demonstrate them through your actions.

In any job application or interview an F1 team will be looking for evidence of what personal qualities you have which can help them as they strive to move up the grid and outperform their rivals. A resume which shows only a set of school grades (be they good or bad) does not tell them much about your personal qualities. The things that you do outside of formal education are the vehicle you must use to convey the personal qualities that you have developed along the way.

What are the critical qualities that F1 teams need and why are they also important though? This chapter will attempt to describe some of those skills and why they are so sought after in an F1 environment.

1)   The ability for quick thinking

In Formula 1 time stops for no one and almost everything that you do is a race against time. There is often an image of Formula 1 people being deep thinkers and whilst there are many long term projects that happen in racing, the vast majority of F1 takes place under extreme time pressure.

At the circuit or at the factory there is often no time to fully consider every option and the ability to make a decision quickly and come up with a solution to unexpected problems is a valuable skill. School is normally based on long term learning and a test of recollection and so there a few opportunities to show this. Situations where you have been put on the spot and had to act on gut instinct are the times where you are put to the test. Real racing experience is ideal to help you develop because this is kind of reactive situation crops up in almost all types of racing.

2) Determination

This is perhaps one of the most critical skills required both to get to and then exist in Formula 1. Life is rarely straightforward and knock backs or difficulties along the way to your goals are almost inevitable. You demonstrate your true qualities when you deal with the difficult times rather than how you ride the good times.

F1 is full of difficult times, even when you are a winning team. The confidence and determination required to keep trying and striving when events are conspiring against you is a highly valued personal quality in Formula 1. If you can demonstrate that you have come back from disappointment and succeeded in your goals even when you have been turned away or have failed at your first attempts you will be showing potential employers that have a very valuable personal quality. Success is not all about getting things right first time as even the very best people learn through their mistakes.

3) Cooperation and Teamwork

F1 is a team sport both at the races and at the factory. Nearly everything that you do will depend in part on the input of others and so the ability to cooperate and work within a team is vital. School learning has traditionally been a solo endeavour where you are marked on your own personal ability to answer questions and recall facts. Project work attempts to teach you the skills required to work in a group and is extremely important in developing the ability to cooperate. In F1 you will need to work with all manner of different people with different educational backgrounds, ages and agendas and so extra-curricular experience is again very good at giving you a wider insight into how to work within a team. You will need to show that you can compromise where necessary and yet show leadership and determination where required.

4) Competitive Drive

As we discussed earlier in the book, there is actually very little core purpose to Formula 1 outside of the competition and desire to win. To go the extra mile and push yourself to achieve in this arena you should enjoy the sport for the competitive elements as much as the technical or commercial aspects. If you are satisfied with second place then you are unlikely to push yourself to your maximum. It is amazing what someone can achieve when they are driven by desire even compared to someone who inherently has greater ability or experience but who is not so motivated.

Sport of any kind is the ideal vehicle for showing your competitive side, even solo events such as running or cycling. Motorsport in particular can demonstrate that you enjoy the fight of competition, driving you to improve both yourself and your equipment. Given the expense of racing, nobody truly does it just for fun, it is all about winning and F1 teams love to employ people who are driven to succeed.

5) Inquisitive and questioning

A common trait of all successful Formula 1 people is the need to constantly improve. This is driven by determination and a competitive nature of course but it is channelled into an inquisitive mind and the need to find out more and to learn. The more that you can understand and the more knowledge you can gather, the better placed you will be to use that to your advantage.

Despite what the popular press may have you believe, nobody truly understands racing cars very well. There is a vast amount that we do not understand and have not yet fully exploited. It is one of the fascinating aspects of the sport. The people who accept this and crave to dig deeper and understand more are typically the people who are the most inventive as they have their eyes open to new ways of thinking and solving problems. It's a cliché but the more I have learned about racing cars the more I realise I don't know.

Sadly, I see many young engineers or graduates who think they "know it all" but nothing could be further from the truth. Confidence is one thing but you should use this to relish new challenges not to sit on your laurels. Be prepared to learn again and again.

6) Clear communication

Time pressure in Formula 1 governs many aspects of what we do and as with any difficult technical arena the ability to clearly convey an idea or instruction with the minimum of confusion or doubt is critical. You often do not get a second chance to correct yourself or clarify details and so the ability to describe the essential components of a task or new idea is essential.

This clarity applies to both verbal and written communications. When you apply for a job your CV, resume and covering letter are the primary test of this ability as you need to convey your qualifications, skills and motivations and sales pitch to the reader as concisely as you can. If you do a poor job of this then you will not normally get a second chance to convince them and the same is true when you enter the world of work.

7) Creativity and Inventiveness

As anyone who follows Formula 1 will appreciate, invention and creativity is the essence of producing a competitive or winning racing car. The ability to do things better, create new techniques and see opportunities where others do not is the key to improvement whether that is in the car's design, operationally or to create new commercial opportunities. It is debatable whether creativity is a natural gift or something which you can learn but I personally believe that it can be taught and learnt through experience.

At school, you generally do not need to be creative to pass exams, especially within the science and maths realm. Project work and design are generally where these abilities are put to the test and can be developed and it is also why extra-curricular activities such as Formula Student are so valuable. As I will discuss later in the book however the most beneficial lessons are found where you seek out your own solutions to real problems which you come across. Solving a need is the essence of any creativity and if that need is driven by the desire to overcome a difficulty or lack of competitiveness in racing or other competition then you have the most to gain. These are the skills and experiences that Formula 1 teams love to see in their potential employees and you should seek them out and make the most of them.

8) Never being satisfied

Adrian Newey and Ross Brawn are typically the two most well known and successful technical directors of the last 2 decades. They each have undoubted technical abilities and clearly understand what it takes to create a quick racing car but it is another attribute that I most admire in these and several other successful individuals. The relentless drive that comes from never being satisfied is what has allowed these people to continue to excel year on year despite enormous success. It would be so easy for them to collect their championship trophies and walk away from the sport but instead they have gone back each year and tried to better themselves and constantly improve. This is motivation that comes from never being satisfied and always believing that you can do a better job tomorrow.

This is common trait in this sport and it is how people really excel. Look at your own CV and achievement and ask yourself are you satisfied and contented? If you are then the chances are you will not progress much further along your journey. If you sit back at any stage then someone else will almost certainly keep going and probably beat you to your unfinished goals. You can always do more and you should constantly strive if you want to win and better yourself even if you have already achieved success.

8) Optimism It's been said many times that most teams in motorsport do a great deal more losing than winning. It must be true as there is only one winner and many more losers on every grid.

Everybody deserves their day in the sun but you might have to wait for some time to get it. Those people who view the world from an optimistic perspective will always believe that their day is just around the corner and are able to motivate themselves to work towards a better future no matter how bad things get. TV coverage concentrates on winners but put yourself in the shoes of a mid-grid or tail-end team and consider how motivated you would be to work hard when success seems so far away. One thing is for sure, without optimism and hard work that success will not get any closer. Making the best of each situation and projecting a positive attitude is tremendously important and optimistic people can lift a team around them and push everyone on to better things.

9) Initiative

Many people are good at following instructions but as we have seen already real improvements and progress come from creativity and inventiveness. A very similar but equally important quality which is much valued in F1 is initiative. We see it so many times where people who wait to be told what to do are never as successful as those who think for themselves and use their own initiative to solve problems or make improvements. It is such a pleasure to manage people who drive themselves on their initiative and exceed expectations rather than having to be led step by step through each task. This is where real team success is born.

When you present your CV for consideration at an F1 team they will looking for evidence that you have used your initiative to organise or get involved in something of your own making rather than simply follow the path that your school or university education has laid down for you. Did you arrange your own work experiences or did the school put you in touch? Did you talk to team and car owners when you went to club/kart races or did you just watch from the side-lines? Look at your own experience and consider whether it shows you use your initiative or whether you just follow the path organised for you. It can make all the difference.

10) A thick skin

This final point is not strictly a skill but it certainly is a personal quality that may be needed for a career in motorsport. Any competitive environment has its challenges and it is not hard to imagine that if you fill such a team or company with skilled and motivated people then conflict will never be far away. For all the talk of teamwork and collaboration there will inevitably be days where the pressure cooker gets too full and aggression takes over. Over the course of my career I have been called far more than my fair share of four letter words, had several car parts and tools thrown at me and have had to give as good as I get in order to keep my head above water.

Motorsport can be a tough place to work if you are easily offended. Most teams work on a sink or swim basis and there is not a lot of support if you do not fit in or pull your weight. Much of the banter is good natured but everyone, good or bad will have to bear the brunt of criticism or practical jokes. Some stories from the track in particular are eye opening, with the removal of hair, dying of skin and immersion in food waste (or worse) not unheard of as jokes at a season end. It's not for the faint hearted and you should at least be prepared for this before you get there and watch your back!

The attributes I have described above are not exclusive to Formula 1 but as I stress throughout this book, life skills are as important as good academic or college qualifications. Your personality and attitude are very hard to demonstrate on a paper application or even at a face to face interview and so this is where your extra-curricular actions and experiences will speak for you. Spending time developing yourself and demonstrating that you have some of these essential skills will stand you in good stead when you do get the opportunity to work in Formula 1.

Part 4 : School Days, University and Education

1 What to study, where and when

Education is a critical part of the preparation required for any demanding career and Formula 1 is no exception. There are many tremendously clever and well qualified people up and down the pitlane and each team seeks to recruit the best and most capable candidates that it can. The goal is to strengthen its line up and get a competitive advantage over its rivals. Without question, people are the most important possession of any F1 team, much more so than any machine or technology. The knowledge, ideas and energy that those people bring to the team are what makes the difference between winning and losing.

We have already touched upon what personal skills Formula 1 demands of you but this section of the book is all about what to study to get the right knowledge and experience behind you for a career in F1. I have stressed how important the extracurricular side of your education is but without doubt you will need a good set of formal qualifications appropriate to your chosen discipline. The more technical the job role that you have decided to go for the more important your academic qualifications will be.

Education is understandably one of the most common areas that I get asked about by aspiring Formula 1 people. It's very easy to think that there is a special education just for Formula 1 but in most cases the subjects and qualifications required are very like other mainstream industries. It is generally just the application of that same knowledge that distinguishes F1 people from other industries.

As you might expect, a good knowledge of engineering and how things work will be critical if you want to make your career in the technical side of the sport but a relevant qualification is also tremendously important if you see your future in marketing, manufacturing or at trackside. This chapter will deal with each area of the industry in turn, look at the different options available and how to build up the necessary knowledge and qualifications as you work your way through school and university if you so choose.

There is no doubt that people who excel at school and university are attractive to Formula 1 teams. We want the very best people that we can get. As we have already touched upon however you do not need straight A grades and a PhD to work in F1. Without a balanced CV and a range of relevant experiences then school grades alone are irrelevant. The ideal candidate is top of their class and runs a successful racing team at weekends but I am yet to meet this perfect person.

For the practical type roles in manufacturing, trackside mechanics and subassembly, your experiences will be far more important than your school grades. In these roles, many of the best people will have left school and started employment immediately to work their way up through the industry. For highly technical jobs such as vehicle dynamics and aerodynamics your education and qualifications will take the front seat and be scrutinised much more carefully. The technical content required by these roles is much higher and so theory and fundamental understanding is more important than practical skills. Here a PhD will be highly valued and those who excel in education will rise to the top.

The best people will always be those who can demonstrate a balance of both but if exams are not your strong point then you should not despair. The diversity of roles in F1 means that there will always be opportunities and you should identify and work to the strengths that you have rather than measure yourself against an unrealistic ideal. Unfortunately, I see many young people who on paper have good or even excellent grades and yet are totally clueless about how that knowledge relates to the real world. They are good at passing exams but do not understand what it is they are learning about or why. Good grades only give us an indication that someone might be promising but often they are less capable than their fellow classmates. It is all about balance and always you should concentrate on convincing us that you have what it takes.

As we will see towards the end of the book there is no fixed or accepted way into Formula 1. No subject, school or university course will guarantee you a job in F1 and it would be foolish to rely on that possibility. Following the advice in this section will get you the most suitable grounding in your chosen area but it won't seal the deal. Choosing your education is perversely one of the easiest things to do along this journey and does not have to follow a rigid path. For now however let's concentrate on school and how to make the best of it.

In part 3 we met Ladbrooke F1, a fictional organisation we used to describe the various job roles within a typical Formula 1 team. We'll be visiting that team again and discussing what qualifications each job role within it would need as they can often differ substantially. I've read several posts on motorsport forums recently where members have confidently pronounced that nearly everyone in an F1 team has a PhD, even the mechanics and the truckies. It's a common misconception that you need to be a born genius to even contemplate working in F1 and these rumours put many people off even trying. I'm glad to say that this is simply nonsense. In fact, I don't know of any jobs in F1 which *require* a PhD and in fact a great deal of them can be carried out very capably by people with little formal education at all.

Let's remind ourselves again of the distinct areas that make up a typical team such as Ladbrooke F1.

- Design & Engineering
- Manufacturing & Assembly
- Marketing & PR
- Business Functions
- The Race team

As we have already seen, the demands of each area can be very different and so the educational backgrounds of the people who work in them are also necessarily quite different. The theoretical intensity of computational fluid dynamics and aerodynamics is vastly different from the patience and practical skill required to laminate a carbon wishbone for example and an individual who excels at one is unlikely to be gifted at the other.

Depending on which area most interests you and what type of work you enjoy doing you will be looking for a different type of education and training. If you want to be a trackside mechanic for example, a PhD would certainly be unnecessary and it would be a waste of time, money and effort attempting to pursue one.

Below, I'll take each area of the team in turn and discuss what is necessary and what the recommended route through education and initial training is. My notes will be based on the UK education system but I expect that those recommendations would transfer to the systems in many other countries very easily. For those outside of the UK our school and university system is typically as follows:

GCSE : General Certificate of Secondary Education

Compulsory examinations following 2 years of study for 14 to 16 year olds. Contains compulsory core subjects but some chosen subjects by the pupil. Pupils can then leave school age 16.

A-Level : Advanced Level

A further 2 year period of voluntary study for ages 16-18. Typically made up of

3 or 4 pupil selected subjects, used as qualifying or selection criteria for university study.

University

A 3 year minimum specialisation in a single discipline leading to either a Bachelor's or Master's degree. Typically for students in their early 20's.

Postgraduate Study

Further specialisation or in depth learning. Any age once an undergraduate degree has been obtained. Sometimes taken following a period of work.

Hopefully with an understanding of the above basic structure and the descriptions below you would be able to find equivalent levels or institutions which can offer you the same training. To return to Ladbrooke F1 therefore, let us start with the most popular subject for aspiring Formula 1 people.

Design & Engineering

This area of the team is one of the most common job roles that I am asked about either in person or via my jobinf1.com blog. It's the area that I work in and it is also the one which makes up the most significant proportion of any team pay roll. Engineering is also making somewhat of a fashionable come back in the UK and there are now many Science, Technology, Engineering & Maths (STEM) initiatives to help young people learn and get experience of practical engineering. (Take a look at www.nationalstemcentre.org.uk to learn more). It is certainly an area which the education system is supporting heavily and attempting to encourage more individuals to get involved in.

There are always exceptions but typically anyone who wishes to join the design office or become an aerodynamicist in Formula 1 should be aiming to get a university degree either in mechanical or aeronautical engineering. In days gone by, it was possible to "work your way up" and become a designer after serving as a mechanic or shop floor technician but in today's world that is becoming increasingly difficult. It certainly would not be the quickest way to get there and I think this route will be all but unheard of in the future. It's not something that I would recommend you attempt to do at the outset.

If you are set on engineering and design as a career then I have some very good news for you. For these types of roles, the subjects you need to study and the route you need to take through education is very clear and well trodden. There are no secrets or special tuition required just because it is F1. The fundamentals required for any engineering role are always the same and you will have a very similar background to most other engineers even though you want to specialise in Formula 1.

The key thing to remember about learning for engineering is that it is a very traditional subject. The rules that govern the way the world works do not change with the times and have been well understood for centuries. New technologies may come along (and F1 is full of them) but your ability to create and develop these new technologies is dependent on you understanding some very fundamental principles. It's what you then go on to do with those principles that lead to the new technologies. In my experience, the best engineers are those who excel at these fundamentals and can break down complex problems into very simple ones. As the famous quote suggests "Simplicity is the ultimate sophistication" and in F1 this holds very true.

I make this point about a traditional education because from the outside, Formula 1 can appear very specialist. It's common for people to believe that there must be a unique or specialist course or qualification that is required in order to get in. It follows that if you don't have this qualification then you can't get in. Frustration leads many to believe that this is all part of the secret club. This is not the case at all.

The temptation is for aspiring F1 people to search endlessly for the secret course but if you look at existing F1 people they were educated at all sorts of different institutions. LinkedIn is a great resource for you to check this for yourself. Most engineering courses cover the same principles and to similar standards and so there is no extra specialisation required. It's often difficult for people outside of F1 to believe but it's actually quite straightforward.

The best education you can get is one which gives you a solid grounding in basic engineering to give you that fundamental understanding to fall back upon when you come up against complex real world problems. This is not glamorous, it's not exciting and it may actually be a little bit boring but trust me, it's what you need to do. Textbooks might seem a long way from the pitlane at Monaco but solid traditional engineering principles are what govern how racing cars behave and perform. Learning how to apply those principles is just the final step. You should not be tempted to ignore this or take shortcuts, it will only bite you later.

What makes the difference as to whether you make it to F1 or not will not be your school or which university you choose it is the things you do *outside* of education and in the real world to back up your fundamental learning. Successful F1 engineers are generally those who have a traditional engineering qualification from a respected university but who back that up with real world racing experience and demonstrate initiative and drive to make their own opportunities outside of school. These people are few and far between but I'll discuss some examples in Part 6. For now, let's stick to education, here are my recommendations:

At GCSE and especially at A-Level, core subjects should be Maths and Physics. These subjects are the fundamental requirement behind all engineering specialisms and a good grounding in both subjects will be essential as you move on to University.

Beyond Maths and Physics you should ideally choose another Science, Technology, Engineering & Maths (STEM - take a look at www.nationalstemcentre.org.uk) related subject of your choice. This could be another science, computing, design and technology or even economics or business. Foreign languages are not essential for engineering but motorsport is very international with strong industries in Germany and Italy amongst others so I would choose one of these two if you feel that language is a strong point of yours.

Design & Technology (D&T) is ideal for teaching you the same ideas and concepts that F1 engineers use in everyday work as they develop new parts and systems to make their cars go faster. I would recommend that you study D&T or another creative subject that your school may offer such woodwork or electronics, especially if it complements a specialism that you have in mind. The opportunity for project work in these types of subjects gives you the chance to integrate a racing application into your study and begin building a portfolio of unique and interesting achievements for your CV.

At university, the choice is again quite clear. The traditional nature of engineering means that a plain mechanical engineering degree from a reputable and well respected university will be the best choice. If you are certain that you want to be involved in aerodynamics then an aeronautical engineering degree will probably be a better choice for that direction but again you should choose as reputable a university as your A-level grades will allow you to. I'll discuss more on how to choose the *right* university in a following chapter.

Most courses will allow you to take a year off your studies to do a work placement as part of your course and I would suggest that this should be a high priority. Many, if not all F1 teams offer work placements at the time of writing and they are golden opportunities to get your foot in the door and start your career even before you have completed your degree. I can't emphasise enough how important these types of scheme can be to your future career.

The competition for these places is rightly fierce but it's amazing how many people claim never to have seen the advert on team websites and miss the opportunity completely. Many of them are open from the start of the academic year so do not leave it until the summer approaches as you will have let this opening slip by. It's one of the reasons why you need to be ready even before you finish your degree with as many extra-curricular activities as possible which can make you attractive to the teams. It is no good waiting and relying on a good degree mark at the end because many graduate jobs are filled by those who took the work placements and so you will kick yourself if you miss out on this opportunity. I would start planning and working on building a strong application even whilst you are still at school. We will discuss these schemes again later in the book.

Manufacturing & Assembly

The educational route for the hands on disciplines of manufacture and assembly is a little different from that required for design & engineering. The academic content of these jobs is less demanding than for degree level engineering and the emphasis shifts towards practical skill and an understanding of how things are made and how they are put together. It is not likely that you would need or even benefit from a university degree if you wished to work in this area.

As we saw in the previous section, the route through school for engineers is well defined and the choices for subject to follow are very simple. For the more practical areas of manufacturing and assembly however it is less well defined as there are not to my knowledge specific courses that will give you the skills and experience that you require in these roles. The emphasis will lie more in your college course and your work experience.

Needless to say, a practical element in your school education such as woodwork, metalwork, design and technology or any kind of craft work would be useful for nurturing and developing the hands on skills and understanding of materials that you will rely on later. A good grasp of maths would be a definite advantage and the basic sciences if you are so inclined.

As you work your way through school, the things you do outside of school will be important (as is always the case) such as building and repairing bikes, old cars or borrowing a neighbour's welding equipment. Go out, look and seek ways to learn about making things and how machines and such are put together. Buy a tool kit and use it. These skills are things that text books cannot teach you.

Beyond the age of 16 when compulsory schooling in the UK finishes you have a number of options. An apprenticeship is ideal and many F1 teams offer, them giving experience in all areas of their company before yourself and the team decide where your best skills lie and what the business needs are at that time for a permanent job. It's the best training that there is as you will learn from the experience of the older technicians and see first hand what it is you are aiming for. Look at the team websites for details (early as places are very limited) or check out www.apprenticeships.org.uk.

RICHARD LADBROOKE

This is an extract from the Williams F1 team apprentice scheme:

Exciting opportunities are available based at our headquarters in Grove, Oxfordshire. This is suited to enthusiastic individuals who have a passion for engineering, along with the confidence, belief and determination to succeed in a company that offers variety, interest and responsibility with great engineering prospects for the future.

As part of the training apprentices will, in addition to attending College, rotate throughout the Metallic and Composite Production areas of the business. Within a fast moving environment of diverse technical challenges, they will learn to interpret technical drawings plus use a variety of materials and techniques. They will therefore develop a good range of hand crafting skills, as well as the ability to measure and fit components accurately. Ultimately, they will progress through the apprenticeship to take up roles within the Composites and Model Shop departments.

Applicants for these positions should be committed to pursuing vocational qualifications in engineering and will receive support accordingly from the Company during the term of the apprenticeships. Applicants are expected to have a good standard of education at GCSE level including Maths and English at grade C or above and have good communication skills. A flexible attitude to work and hours is essential, as well as being a good team player.

If you cannot get a Formula 1 apprenticeship then look around the wider motorsport industry, do your research, go where the masses do not follow and find your own. If you must take an apprenticeship outside of racing then so be it, the lessons will be just as valuable but that will only intensify the need to get your racing experience in your own time. Relevancy is the key and showing your commitment to racing through the choices you make and the things that you get involved in outside of school and work will make or break you.

If you decide to stay on in full time education or cannot get an apprenticeship then there are several relevant options for you. Many colleges around the country offer City & Guilds, BTEC (Business and Technology Education Council) or HNC (Higher National Certificate) courses in Vehicle Technology, Motorsport or Mechanical Engineering. There are a great number of these courses available, too many to mention but there are no real stand-out "must do" courses that closely associate with the motorsport industry more than the others. The options are changing all the time and so I would recommend that you just do as much research as you possibly can.

The modules and skills taught will vary but all will likely have good relevancy to motorsport. The key thing is to maintain a link to racing either directly through your studies or ideally through your extracurricular activities. If you get the opportunity to practice what you are learning then take it, the experience you get will quickly overtake the value of your qualifications and indeed your certificate is likely to be nearly irrelevant once you have established yourself in the sport. Whatever you chose to study, do not rely on it 100% to get you a job - it will not and so you must only consider you college qualifications as part of your skill set.

A relatively new initiative in the motorsport arena are dedicated technical colleges which are government funded institutions teaching scientific and technical subjects to 14-18 year olds. They offer the chance to specialise in STEM subjects at an earlier age and as such can offer greater detail and experience of industry and some of the skills required than an ordinary secondary school.

In terms of motorsport Silverstone UTC (www.utc-silverstone.co.uk) is one of the first University Technical Colleges to open nationwide. It claims to provide a unique curriculum dedicated to training and educating the future workforce of the Motorsport industry. Being situated directly outside the gate of the country's premier circuit you would certainly have a good vantage point for what happens at race meetings. From what I understand they have already forged links with several motorsport teams and suppliers and have organised talks from key people in the industry. Time will tell whether it is a total success but it is certainly an interesting development which will expose you to the motorsport industry early on and help you understand how it works and the job roles on offer.

In a similar vein the National College for Motorsport (www.nc4m.ac.uk) offers motorsport specific courses for students aged 16 and older. It gives candidates the chance for hands on learning with real racing cars and has established excellent industrial links. It was awarded the Motorsport Academy Employer Recognition Scheme Charter Mark for its training of race mechanics.

Several universities are also now offering motorsport specific courses but this is something I will discuss as part of a dedicated chapter on University Choices later in the book.

With all of these choices you must remember however that these are not golden tickets to a job by themselves. You must continue to seek you own experiences and boost your skills outside of college where you are able. You are in competition with everyone including your course mates and if the college course is all you have to show then it will be hard to tell you apart from your peers. Consider that there will be other colleges offering similar courses and that a new class graduates each year, you are in danger of being lost in the crowd. Your qualifications are rarely enough on their own.

Marketing & PR

Some people will tell you that F1 is not a sport at all but simply a mass marketing exercise. I'm not sure I'd go that far but marketing and the economic activity it generates is certainly a central theme to any form of motor racing as expensive as Formula 1.

This aspect of the business is quite different to the technical side of the sport and I won't claim to be an expert. If I were to be asked to pitch to potential sponsors or host any kind of event I would fall flat very quickly. It is certainly not a career for me. I do find it fascinating however and to see how some of the senior marketing people operate is quite an education. It is a real skill there is no doubt.

Most account managers in marketing these days will be degree qualified and this is certainly what you should be aiming to do if you are serious about getting to F1. Numerous institutions offer Marketing & Business degrees but this career is still open to you from a range of qualified backgrounds such as Politics, Economics and even History. Marketing is best suited to well rounded individuals who are presentable and able to communicate and express themselves confidently. These qualities are important to maintain high level business and personal relationships with clients. Whilst academic qualifications are important, be wary of appearing *too* academic. Persuading somebody to part with large sums of money to allow people like us to go motor racing is about engaging with people and understanding their needs, how to serve them and get them greatest value for their investment.

Most universities want to see a diverse background in your school subjects, not just pure business or science and not just the humanities. This is where your well-rounded personality needs to start. This is an extract from Bath University's prospectus :

We have a strong preference for applicants with qualifications that demonstrate a breadth and depth of learning, which includes a combination of mathematics/sciences, with arts/humanities.

Candidates offering the following types of narrow subject combinations are less likely to receive an offer:

Business Studies and Economics Accounting and Business Studies English Literature and English Language Mathematics and Further Mathematics.

Once again, your extracurricular activities speak as loudly as you school grades. If your school is organising an end of year celebration, get involved, ask a local company to sponsor the event and be at the front choosing venues and organising the catering. At university you should be involved in societies, it doesn't matter what overall but offer to be on the committee, campaign to be on the student union or head of your hall of residence sports team.

Networking is critical within this industry and opportunities for many sponsorship deals in F1 start from contacts, leads and referrals. Learning this skill and building your contacts should start as early as possible and if you are able you should use your contacts to get your first job. Go to trade shows, both racing and marketing and go to the races and talk to people, be it racers or event organisers. Offer your services (for free) if you get the chance, who knows you could even bring some marketing income to a friend or acquaintance that races at the weekends. If you can do that at this level then you can do it in F1 and it will show on your CV. Many junior drivers and karters have no kind of PR or marketing backing and if you were to walk up to one of these people and offer to help them then they are likely to bite your hand off. Work for them, learn about the frustration of being turned down time after time and build up the skills, ideas and resolve required for this business. Any material you produce for those individuals can form a portfolio for university applications and job applications and will carry substantial weight as they are from the real world rather than just a theoretical exercise. How about starting a social media campaign for your local racer? Opportunities are there, you just need to get out there and make a start.

Marketing a two-way transaction, in fact it should be more about the client than you. Don't think of it as begging, consider what positives sponsorship can offer and use your imagination devising ways that the client can benefit from it. Don't ask for money, you should propose a deal which benefits everybody.

One of the key aspects to this job is being used to dealing with clients, working for them and understanding their needs. Typically a junior marketing account manager would be involved in liaison, event organisation and sponsor days first of all to get them used to being on show, representing the team and understanding what clients want and need from their association with the team. I see many junior marketing people giving factory tours, hosting clients on pitlane walkabouts and at driver signings. They are there to enhance the client experience and be customer facing. By so doing they learn to put themselves in the shoes of sponsors and to understand what they want and need from a partnership with a motor racing team. Every form of hosting is valuable in this way and if you look through LinkedIn at some of the career histories of F1 marketing people you will see many of them have carried out events management in sport or other industries first as they try and break into Formula 1. Even waitering is a valuable starting point for your customer facing experience.

Look at the Chartered Institute of Marketing - www.cim.co.uk for more ideas or look at the educational background of F1 marketing people on LinkedIn.

Business Functions

For all the talk so far about how tough it can be to get an engineering or marketing job, I would say that in fact, the day to day business functions within an F1 team are probably the most difficult positions to get into.

I say that, not because they are particularly different to an internal business role in other industries, require hard to get qualifications or a particular work history but because they require none of those things. Compared to engineering jobs and marketing roles they are few and far between as they make up a relatively small percentage of the team workforce. They are in effect more specialist than these other roles and this is in fact why they are so difficult to get.

F1 teams employ lots of engineers and as I have tried to advise, there is a well-worn path you need to follow to get there. For jobs such as accountancy, IT and logistics however there is little that you can do at school to increase your chances of landing one of these jobs. The route is the same as it would be for that same discipline in any other company as the content of the job is also very similar. The company note paper just happens to say F1 at the top.

That's not to say that you can't make yourself attractive to F1 through your extra-curricular activities and the same rules apply about getting out and getting involved in racing. You may not need to convince your paymasters quite so hard that you are dedicated for Formula 1 but it cannot harm. Your work history and experience should certainly show the willing and commitment that all jobs in Formula 1 can sometimes demand.

Whilst there is not much more I can say on the subject, you should read on and pay attention to the later chapters on how to gain extra-curricular experience and using the stepping stones and racing ladder to work your way into F1. An enthusiasm and knowledge of the motorsport world and the industry behind it will be your best weapon as you seek out an opening for your career.

The Race Team

Again, I have left the section until last even though I know that this part of an F1 team is that which many of you will see as your ultimate target. As you will have seen from the section "A typical F1 team and the people who work in it" the race team has a diversity of roles which represent a cross section of the team as a whole. The advice here is therefore a mixture of what I have said in the previous paragraphs.

As such, the choices you make at school will very much depend on which role within the race team you wish to follow. The mechanics will for example have very different backgrounds, education and work histories to the data engineers and strategists.

For those of you who wish to be an engineer, the same advice applies as that I gave for design and engineering at the beginning of this chapter. Increasingly the race and data engineers within the race team will have served their time as vehicle dynamicists at the factory and will be degree qualified in mechanical engineering. Some may have worked in another high level race series prior to F1 and will have arrived via the racing ladder. This is one of the few engineer jobs remaining where this gives you valid experience but is becoming less and less common.

Trackside aerodynamics is becoming ever more important but the same rules apply as these engineers will also be time served back at the factory having used their aeronautical engineering degree to first prove themselves in the windtunnel environment. The need for trackside aerodynamics engineering is much lower in other formulas so it is unlikely that they would use this racing ladder approach. The same is true of strategists except for experienced gained in high level endurance racing such as Le Mans or American racing in IndyCar or NASCAR.

The mechanics and truckies on the race team may well have served an apprenticeship or similar before deciding that they wanted to travel and work as a junior mechanic. Many of the race team mechanics will however have worked elsewhere within the industry prior to F1, gathering experience in GP2, sports cars or other high level race series. Their education will be very similar to that I described for Manufacturing & Assembly earlier but they have used the racing ladder to gather experience once they have entered the world of work. Again, understanding the industry and working your way up is vital and this is where some of the motorsport specific college courses offer real advantage as they have excellent industrial links. Simply by being involved with a race team at any level you will quickly understand how the wider industry works and meet a variety of people who can advise you. Education is important but experience is key in whatever form you can get it and this should be your focus if you see yourself in one of these hands on roles.

As we have already discussed you don't need a PhD to work in every job in Formula 1. Throughout this book, I have also emphasised that it is the things that you do outside of work and education that will give you the best chance of working in F1.

Having said all that, you may be left wondering whether you need to go to school at all or can just spend all your days at the race track. I wish that were true but sadly it isn't. There is no doubt that your formal education is still an essential ingredient in your training for Formula 1 and to ignore it totally would be foolish. The more academic your target job role, such as vehicle dynamicist and aerodynamicist, the more emphasis and scrutiny will be placed on your performance at school and university. If you have failed all of your exams you will not be able to get yourself into one of these jobs roles no matter how keen you are. Even for more vocational candidates your education record will still be looked at closely and you will need to do achieve some very impressive things outside of school to offset a poor academic record. F1 teams want exceptional and talented people and will compare you against the best. As always, it's a balance of your talents.

I wasn't top of my class. I'm not afraid to say it and I manage people today who I consider to be more intelligent than I am. I recognised this fact quite early on, especially at university and I slogged my guts out to meet the required standards. I worked much harder than many of the people who got higher grades than I did and sacrificed more. I'm proud of my results and they are certainly better than average but they were not the best in the class. It hasn't held me back however because I did other things besides school and when put alongside each other they formed a good candidate (I think).

The purpose of this book is not to tell you how to do well at school or to help you to pass exams. I'm consciously leaving that to text books and teachers. The more you can do in that arena the better and I won't tell you that you don't need good grades. The reason the emphasis in this book is on what to do outside of school is because this is where I think there is a lack of advice, especially in motorsport where it is so important. What I wanted this book to be is a parallel guide to your formal education and give you the advice you need on how to complement a set of good exam grades. We get lots of candidates with good grades but with little else to show. Clearly the education system is working in that regard but it doesn't provide that specific motorsport experience and knowledge that teams crave. At the risk of repeating myself too many times you need to strike a balance and push every part of your education as far as you are able both formal and extra- curricular. Only you can decide how to get that balance but this book exists to give you the viewpoint from within the industry.

We will discuss working your way through that industry later in the book and I hope then you will be able to see where education and work experience can come together.

2 F1 in Schools and other education initiatives

In the previous chapter we saw that at school level at least, it is very difficult to choose subjects or a specialist education which will prepare you directly for F1. School is (for good reasons too) mainly about teaching you some fundamentals and giving you the backbone of skills which you will need to prepare you for university or for a working life. It is essential that you just knuckle down and get the best grades that you can before you specialise.

Outside of the classroom is normally where you need to gather race and motorsport specific experience and to nurture the creative and clear thinking aspects of your personality. In recent years however, several initiatives have started which allow a standard school curriculum to be combined or channelled through a motorsport related competition or theme. These are a fantastic first introduction to how the industry operates and will tell you a great deal about yourself and what you might enjoy in the world of work.

This chapter will be about how to get involved and make the most of those opportunities using some of the most popular schemes.

Greenpower Trust

http://www.greenpower.co.uk

Having started in 1999, the Greenpower Trust works with 500 schools and 8000 pupils, organising events and initiatives that allows pupils to design, build and race a variety of electric powered cars. There are strict regulations to follow but the variety of machines that compete show the creativity and invention that children of this age can bring to such a competition. The thought processes, difficulties, challenges and rewards are incredibly like those which we experience in Formula 1 but Greenpower allows pupils to experience this and develop their skills in a fun and accessible team environment where they get to meet children from different schools and backgrounds.

It encourages original thought, creative design and competitive rivalry amongst school age children. It also allows them to channel their STEM based learning into a real and rewarding activity and bring their classroom studies to life.

The series is sponsored and supported by several large businesses including several motorsport companies like Prodrive and MSV and is recognised by many motorsport teams as being a valuable and relevant training ground for young engineers.

The hugely popular Goodwood Festival of Speed event which takes place each summer in Sussex and is attended by motorsport figures and teams from all over the world is organised by Earl of March who is also a supporting patron of the Greenpower Trust. He is keen to see young engineers get involved in motorsport and says the following.

"I became the Patron of Greenpower in 2004. As someone heavily involved in motorsport I realise how important it is that this country continues to produce engineers of the highest quality. The Greenpower project is a key part of promoting engineering in schools. Combine this with the current relevance of 'green' transport, and it is clear that Greenpower is an initiative that really works. I look forward to playing a part in its future success."

The Earl of March, Patron of Greenpower

The Institute of Engineering and Technology (IET) http://www.theiet.org are also a primary supporter as well as Siemens who provide their computer aided design (CAD) software free of charge to all competing schools and clubs.

The series is mainly entered into by schools but is also open to youth clubs. Competitions exist for the following age ranges.

- IET Formula Goblin (9-11 years) for primary schools.
- IET Formula 24 (11-16 years old) for secondary schools, youth groups etc.
- IET Formula 24+ (16-25 years old) a fantastic opportunity for 6th forms, colleges, apprentices and universities.

For more information contact the Greenpower Trust at:

Greenpower
The Greenpower Centre
Arundel Road
Fontwell
West Sussex
BN18 0SD
or via their website.

National Schools Karting Association

https://www.facebook.com/natskakarting

Karting has been the entry point into racing for almost every successful F1 driver of the past 2 decades and it continues to be one of the most cost effective ways to learn the art of driving. Junior drivers can spend many seasons in karting honing their craft so that when they finally make the leap up into single seaters they are already very experienced racing drivers. Cost effective it may be in comparison to other forms of circuit racing but it still is not cheap compared to tennis or football. A national championship level season of racing with a privately owned kart can easily run to well over £10,000 and even more if you employ a team or mechanic to run the outfit for you. If you wish to see just how serious karting can be check out:

http://www.superoneseries.com

http://www.cikfia.com/home.html

The National School's Karting Association however is a grass roots form of karting that is much more accessible. It has existed in the UK for well over 30 years and provides a much cheaper entry point into motorsport than running your own kart in the aforementioned championships. A comprehensive class structure allows everyone from 10 year olds with a homemade chassis and a motorbike engine running on second hand tyres to high performance national class karts to compete on full outdoor racing circuits and to get involved with machine maintenance and repair. The racing on track is just as fierce but the cost is shared both with the school or youth club and amongst the other members of the club.

Many people will simply not have space at home for a kart and all the kit required to run one nor could they afford a van or trailer to transport it to race meetings. The use of school workshops and facilities both during school and after hours can give a school age child that valuable first insight to racing and the competitive dedication required to succeed. Many schools and local area clubs run their own practice and race meetings on private land with circuits made of old car tyres reducing costs even further.

If your school is not a current member of NatSKA then discuss the possibility with them or contact NatSKA to find your nearest youth club or school that is involved. Why not go along to one of their meetings and offer to help out. This could be where it all starts.

Bloodhound SSC

Not strictly a motorsport initiative but it has all the same high technology and small team requirements that a motorsport project would have. It is also highly innovative and daring compared to many modern day challenges. The governance and legality of the land speed record is also held by the FIA, the same group that sets the technical regulations for Formula 1.

The land speed record was hotly contested over numerous decades in the mid-20th century but has moved to such incredible velocities that only very serious and well organised groups can now even consider an attempt. Thrust SSC currently holds the World Land Speed Record, set on 15 October 1997, when it achieved a speed of 1,228 km/h (763 mph) and became the first car to officially break the sound barrier. To give you some idea of the achievement, that record is significantly faster than most passenger aircraft.

The same group is now attempting to smash their own record and create a car capable of over 1000mph. They also hope to use that project to generate interest in the UK's STEM capabilities and to inspire the next generation of young engineers. If that speed target is met it will be a truly astonishing achievement.

http://www.bloodhoundssc.com/education

One of the key aims of the bloodhound project has been to use the project to promote science and technology in education and to share the benefits and excitement that such a project can bring with young people. The bloodhound website details a host of curriculum suggestions and projects that can be carried out in schools at all sorts of levels to use the project to promote understanding of STEM related subjects.

Not only that but the group have organised a roadshow, school visits and tours of their technical centre to allow youngsters to get involved and see what the project involves first hand. They are also a centre point for organising work placements and year in industry placements at their supplier and partner companies for interested students.

F1 in Schools

www.f1inschools.com

F1 in Schools is a not-for-profit initiative started back in 1999 which allows school children aged 9-19 to use computer aided design (CAD) and real life manufacturing to create scale model racing cars. The cars are powered by pressurised carbon dioxide canisters and are raced head to head along 20m long tracks. The cars can cover that distance in just over 1 second.

F1 in Schools is now a global competition and brings together children from over 40 countries and international backgrounds. It has been recognised by educational institutions for the role that it plays in developing the talents and abilities of potential future engineers whilst creating a fun and challenging environment where they learn valuable life skills.

The teams who can progress through their regional and national competitions will get the chance to attend the World Finals event which takes place at the final F1 Grand Prix of each year and is judged by some of the leading names from Formula 1. They will also be granted exclusive access to the F1 circuit and paddock with a VIP pit lane tour. It's a fantastic opportunity.

Any school can register and each will be supplied with free design and computational fluid dynamics (CFD) software to start designing their car. A host of classroom material is also available to use the competition as a focal point for a range of lessons and subjects.

Formula E school series

In a very similar initiative to F1 in schools, the Formula E electric series has created an inter-school competition in each of the countries which the series visits during the season.

http://www.fiaformulae.com/en/news/2014/december/fe-school-series.aspx

It is early days as the project is so new but I am sure that this will be a beneficial competition for learning and applying your skills.

Your Own Project Work

Whilst the groups and initiatives mentioned above allow children to join in and learn through organised schemes and programmes it is still possible to bring motorsport into school based learning though your own initiative. Many STEM based subjects at both GCSE and A-Level have individual and group project work where the subject matter is free for pupils to choose provided that it covers the core scope of the subject in question.

I have chosen to put this category at the end of the section but that is not because these types of project are less valuable than the industry backed initiatives mentioned thus far. In my opinion the exact opposite is in fact true. The organised schemes have all proven to be a great introduction to engineering and allow students to get involved but projects brought to life through *your own* initiative will be the most beneficial of all and of greatest interest to potential employers. They demonstrate individual and original thought and require much greater level of perseverance and personal will power than is required to take part in a scheme organised by your school or an outside body.

Computer Science, Product Design or Technology modules often have large weighting attached to design and make type projects where you are free to develop a device or system which fulfils a need in the real world. The scope for ideas is endless but combining this work with motorsport is ideal if you race yourself, have a family member who races or have made contacts with someone in your local area. The key is talking to them and discussing how they work and deciding between you what you can do to make their life quicker and easier. All successful design is based on finding a problem or a real life need and then producing a solution which can solve that need.

For example, I was lucky enough to be able to race karts during my teens and I used this as the basis of several design and make projects. A common issue with the type of 2- stroke karts that I raced was breaking down on the dummy grid or on the warm up lap because the spark plug became too wet with oil before it had a chance to get up to racing temperature. More than once I was left stranded at the side of the track unable to take the start because I had "oiled-up". My solution was to carry a spare plug and plug socket attached to my seat and so I made a moulded cradle that held the tools securely for safety reasons but allowed me to quickly get to them to change the plug on track and potentially still make the start. It was hardly rocket science but it worked and was my first introduction to design. Most importantly it was my own invention.

At A-Level I took this several steps further and developed a prototype dashboard and lap timer for my kart that allowed me to compare my laps from one to the next, triggered with a steering wheel mounted button each time I crossed the line. It meant that I could see how I and the kart were performing real-time without the need for someone to stand trackside and time me. This was before the days when these devices were commercially available and before karts carried transponders linked to each circuit's own timing system. It was simple and a bit agricultural by modern standards but it allowed me to develop my design skills, learn about the process of making something and (as I was told later) showed the initiative and creativity that helped get me my first job in racing.

You may not be involved in racing yet but I hope you can see how experiences can build on one another. It's so important just to make a start, no matter how simple or low level as it opens doors to the next level and so on and so forth. Without the experience I had of racing, I would not have been able to focus my project work so carefully. The fact that I did this however helped me get on my degree course and ultimately was recognised and taken seriously by other race teams that I got involved with. It's hard to go straight from nothing to Formula 1 but there are so many small scale opportunities in between if you just go out and look for them.

This kind of work can often have the greatest benefits when it comes to applying for work placements or full-time jobs because the work you do in setting up and creating the project will likely be recognised more than the project results themselves. It can be anything you like, the subject is probably not important but the fact that you did it carries real weight. It shows exactly the kind of initiative that Formula 1 teams crave in their employees. We'll cover more about this and the other things that school cannot teach you later in this section of the book.

3 University choices

I'm often asked which is the best university to go to if you want to work in F1. The right education and qualifications are clearly very important but is it just about knowledge or do teams favour certain courses or universities over others? It is a complex question and one which many people seemingly agonise over. This chapter attempts to explain my thoughts on the subject and to pass on recommendations on choosing the best university if you want to work in Formula 1.

If you are considering a university education to boost your chances of a career in F1 then you are most likely looking to be a designer, race engineer, vehicle dynamicist or aerodynamicist. A degree can also be important if you want to work in marketing or team management. If you are certain that the university route is for you then the next question is how to choose the university that will prepare you best for your career.

What is the best university for Formula 1 then? Straightaway I'll be honest and say that I can't answer that question. There is no best way, or best university to get into F1. It's just not that simple. If you ask people what the best university in their own country is then you will probably get different answers and opinions and for F1 it is no different. It's certainly subjective and often even an emotive question. What might the best from one person s point of view will almost certainly be different from another's. There is no rule.

There are numerous teams and hundreds of people interviewing candidates for positions so ask yourself would they all have agreed on a best university to take employees from? F1 is a very capitalist open market and rarely has structure or fixed way of doing things and so the idea of a single best university across all teams is very unlikely. Even if there was one, the first thing any thinking team would do would be to break free and hire people from a different university to try to gain an advantage over its rivals. In many cases the best university comes down just to an opinion and I cannot speak for my own team never mind all the others.

The fact that there isn't a single best university to attend which will guarantee you a job in F1 is very good news rather than bad. It may mean that you must do more research rather than just reading this book but what it really means is that you have a decent chance of working in the sport coming from a whole range of different backgrounds. It should be clear if you have done any research into existing F1 people that they have come from a wide variety of previous employments and academic backgrounds and in many different countries. It should also be clear that no-one will be excluded because they did not follow the right path. Having done that research however you can be sure that attending any one of those institutions would not harm your chances of getting into the sport. It's a start and well worth the time spent.

It is of course not entirely random. Certain universities will have good general reputations and others bad. Formula 1 is not unique in this respect as universities will have better or poorer reputations in the wider world not just specifically in motorsport. Oxford and Cambridge Universities in the UK for example are very famous and renowned institutions worldwide and anyone with a good degree from these universities is likely to be regarded as well qualified by another member of the public. This will also apply to a lesser extent to other universities on a sliding scale but the real question is whether these reputations differ or matter within F1? Not an easy question to answer.

I always tell people to try to put themselves in the position of the person who will ultimately be reading their CV or resume when they send in their application. If you worked at an F1 team what would you look for from an applicant's university or other qualifications? F1 engineers are often talented but they don't know everything and are in most respects just very normal people like you or me. Are you likely to know the relative quality of every university across the world and the different courses that they run? No, probably not and neither do many people working at F1 teams. They don't have the time.

What is more likely is that they will have a very similar view of what is a good university and what is a bad university as anyone else. They will make their judgements based on something that they readily understand and is familiar to them. The university that they attended is likely to be near the top of the list but as we have already seen, F1 people come from a wide range of backgrounds and so this doesn't really help unless you happen to be lucky. An individual may hire from the same institution more than once if they are pleased with the quality of people they have already recruited. If you used personal research or something like LinkedIn, this might offer you more information on the academic background of junior engineers but only if you have a very specific team in mind and if your target is as narrow as that then you are likely to be artificially limiting your chances anyway. These trends change too and so by the time you graduate, another university may be in favour and the research was largely wasted.

To help you envisage the process a little more I'm going to use myself as an example. There is only a very small chance that I will be the person who receives your resume if you apply to an F1 team, but I am probably quite typical of the person that does. There are a high percentage of F1 workers from the UK and so there is a high percentage chance that the person that receives your CV was born in, or has worked in the UK at some point. If I use myself as a model therefore, I was born and brought up in the UK, English is my primary language, I have a degree education from a UK university and I graduated around 20 years ago. This might not cover every senior engineer across F1 but there will be some similarities at least. The following are what I might be influenced by when judging what a good university for an F1 applicant might be:

1) The university that I attended for my degree, which is familiar to me
2) The university that my last successful recruitment attended
3) Universities that I or my team have dealt with for research
4) The top 10 universities by general reputation in my home country
5) Universities based in major cities that I recognise from foreign countries around the world

As I mentioned, the individual looking at your application may not fit my description exactly but the scope of what they know and what they understand to be a good university will probably fit the above 5 factors quite closely.

Many F1 recruiters will naturally hire from universities which are known and familiar to them. Given that the largest majority of workers in F1 are European, and a large percentage of them are from the UK then degree qualifications from UK universities are most likely to be recognised and understood in F1. This is not to suggest that UK universities are better than institutions in other countries (statistics do not bear this out anyway) but it is inescapable that they will be more familiar to many of the people who recruit for the teams and so potential candidates in the UK, western Europe or other English speaking countries are most likely at an advantage over other people when it comes to working in F1. This is simply the result of most teams being based in this part of the world.

If you not from the UK but are determined to work in F1 then I would seriously consider coming to the UK to study. This has 2 advantages as it means you will have a qualification which is more readily recognised by the teams and it shows that you are prepared to commit to leaving your home country and happy to travel. As I have discussed elsewhere, commitment and the right mindset are extremely important in any application to an F1 team but demonstrating it can be difficult. A move to a UK university will instantly make you stand out and say something very positive about you to the teams. If you want to work in F1 you will probably have to move to Europe/UK eventually, it might as well be now and is potentially easier at this stage.

I understand however that this kind of move may not always be possible. Financial restrictions are a big consideration for many and visa and passport issues can make such a move difficult for some. If you choose to study in your home country then it will not completely exclude you from a career in F1 (far from it) but you should consider the potential issue of familiarity when it comes to choosing your university. You need to consider the person who is likely to be receiving your application.

If I use myself as an example again, I would be looking for an overseas applicant to have good grades (I may not understand the grading system in your country so consider explaining it in your covering letter) in a relevant subject from a university which I have heard of or from the university of a major city in the country of your residence. For example, I know very little about universities in India, but I would recognise University of Delhi or University of Mumbai as being potentially reputable institutions as they are based in major cities which are internationally recognised. I am less likely to have heard of Vishwakarma Institute of Technology however, even though it may excel in its field. It would be an unknown and inevitably leave some doubt about that application in my mind unless there were other more favourable points in that individual's application. To compare that person to an applicant from a UK university I would need to understand their relative strengths and it would be difficult for me to do this without any knowledge of the other person s qualifications. You could consider a short summary of your university s background and any information that may show its reputation more favourably but do not assume that the reader will know much about where you have studied and they are unlikely to take the time to research it unless you have other stand out qualities in your application.

When I studied for my degree, the choices were blissfully simple. Looking at the range of courses available to aspiring F1 engineers now, things look more confusing. The emergence of motorsport specific degree and college courses has brought the motorsport industry into the mainstream but many young potential F1 engineers are unsure about whether they should be studying one of these newer courses or stick with traditional institutions and subjects. It's a difficult question to answer because as always there are pros and cons to each approach.

A running theme throughout this book has been the need to get out and to get involved in motorsport as early and as much as you can. There is no substitute for real experience. F1 teams are much more likely to employ people who have previous motorsport experience as they know and understand what is required by the job and will have built up skills and knowledge that are essential to meeting the needs of the team.

Getting racing experience isn't easy though. Competing is expensive and even helping out or assisting someone else is time consuming and can cost money. Not everybody is fortunate enough to live in Silverstone or Monza where they can go to races and take in the atmosphere. Privilege or luck, whichever it is, means that not everyone can get involved as easily as the next person. This is tough, but a fact of life.

Without something motorsport related to add to your CV or resume you are destined to join the masses that leave school or graduate from university with nothing other than exam grades and passing interest in Formula 1 to show for it. You might have done well at school but when we receive your application there is little to distinguish you from every other candidate who has also done well in their exams. Why should I pick you over another person who has taken the same exams as you and got the same grades? With nothing more to show you are simply putting your career destiny down to fate or luck.

The advent of motorsport specific college and university courses however has changed things a little and for the better if you are someone who doesn't have a prior background in racing. When I pick up a CV from a candidate who has studied a motorsport specific course I know straightaway that this person knows something about motor racing and has taken their career intentions seriously enough to commit 3 or more years of their life to studying for a job in this industry and this industry alone. That makes you stand out as a more serious candidate.

Being successful in Formula 1 and motorsport is only partly about being clever or inventive. So much of what we do in this sport is about being proactive, dependable, self motivated and dedicated. Your personality is just as important as your qualifications but your exam grades don't tell me anything about your attitude and your work ethic. People can get top marks at school and yet still be totally unsuited to working in F1. When I look at your resume I have no way of knowing anything about your real personality except from your extra-curricular activities. Without a credible list of outside interests and achievements you are unlikely get chosen for an interview.

If I see that you have done a motorsport course however it tells me something about you straight away. I know that you really are interested in racing and that you have gone out of your way to commit to it as early as you could. If you have stuck at that choice, got good grades and are now applying for a job in the industry then you clearly still want it and have ambitions to make it. As a recruiter, I have something more to go on and can separate you out from the pile of otherwise identical CVs I have from other university leavers. There is no doubt you will be more familiar with racing, how the industry works and you may have done courses or modules with content very similar to the actual job content that you will get involved in with a real team. This is all a bonus.

I'll let you into a secret however. I'm not a fan of motorsport specific courses and here is why I think you should still be cautious. First, motorsport courses are starting to be a victim of their own success. At first, they were relatively scarce and so competition existed to get on-board and the number of candidates who completed those courses was small. With so many institutions now offering similar courses, the individuality of the courses is being eroded and the pile of CVs we get from candidates with motorsport specific qualifications is now very large. It's no longer making you stand out from the crowd because you are just the crowd again. It's unfortunate but motorsport courses no longer make you stand out as much as they used to.

Secondly, and this is perhaps controversial, the quality of the institutions that offer these courses is often not as high as the more traditional engineering universities. If you look at universities rated in the top 10 for engineering in the UK, the clear majority do not offer motorsport related courses. These colleges tend to stick to general mechanical and aeronautical degrees and this still carries a great deal of weight in the eyes of many F1 recruiters. In fact, I know several people in the industry who firmly believe that motorsport degrees are no good and that candidates who study for them are generally of a lower standard than those who attend the better regarded institutions.

This of course is not true in every case and I have personally worked with several very, very good engineers who have gone down the motorsport route. Whilst I and many others have reservations, it cannot be denied that there are a great deal of F1 engineers working in the sport today who have gone down this route and it certainly can work. Recruits from Oxford Brookes and Cranfield in particular seem to have a great deal of success and were the institutions that paved the way in this arena and forged the closest ties with F1 and other motorsport companies.

If you are faced with making this choice between a traditional engineering course and a motorsport specific course in the near future then what should you do? The choice is yours but this is my advice: If you have been lucky enough or pro-active enough to collect your own experience in racing and motorsport at school and outside of the classroom then I would recommend that you go to the best university you can and choose a traditional mechanical or aeronautical engineering course. For me, this is the best type of candidate as they have a high quality degree in the fundamentals of engineering and yet they have shown that they have the drive and determination to get experience of racing outside of the normal school system.

If you haven't had that opportunity however or if you have come to motorsport later in your academic life then you risk being anonymous if you get a traditional degree and don't collect motorsport related knowledge as part of your education. The opportunities that the motorsport courses offer are very good and will gave you a real taste of racing before you enter the world of work. For me, it is second best but it is the easiest option for many. Bear in mind however that you will still be in the crowd so it is important to try whatever you can to get yourself ahead of your peers and make yourself unique. Having a motorsport degree will not guarantee you a job in F1 and it would be foolish to rely on that. You can never do enough and so you should always be striving to further yourself and get unique and interesting skills for your resume no matter what courses you have chosen to study.

In summary, your choice of university will not make or break your chances of getting a job in Formula 1 but you should aim to attend the best and most reputable university that you are able to whilst continuing to gather those all important life and motorsport experiences and skills away from the classroom. A degree is just part of your skill set and you will need to make the most of the wider opportunities that it gives you.

4 The things that school cannot teach you

The term "education" has broad meaning but in general it is used to describe formal learning at a school or other academic institution that may lead to exams and a certificate of qualification is some subject or another.

Real life is not all about schools, exams and grades though. Every day you use your experience and intuition to deal with new people, situations and difficulties that you may encounter. You may not realise it much of the time but every day you will be learning and developing skills and attitudes that shape the way you approach life. The greater experience you have of different people and attitudes the more prepared you will be to handle yourself in new situations. When you are faced with a new challenge, the way in which you react and deal with it has little to do with how well you do in exams but is a result of your life experiences. Gathering and demonstrating the right attitude is key to making a career in Formula 1 and in a competitive work situation it can be the difference that gets you the job over another individual.

Modern education is very good in that it can prepare you for the world of work by introducing you to concepts and theories that are necessary to carry out many of jobs that you may wish to pursue as an adult. It is however also very structured and very predictable which is not like real life at all. The world of work can sometimes come as something of a shock to those who have not ventured far beyond the supportive environment of the classroom and home.

As the title and introduction suggest this chapter is not about the formal education system, it is about developing skills for which there are no exams or degrees. Life skills are a difficult thing to define but there is little doubt that they can be as important as your formal education in preparing you for the world of work and especially the world of Formula 1.

We live in a society which is for the most part a civilised one. School should be available to everyone from whatever upbringing or social background they originate. The school system (in the UK at least) is about equality, where each student takes the same exams as their counterparts and the curriculum is defined for each year group. If a child attends school they will be guided and taught along that defined path to maximise their chances of getting good grades in their GCSE or school leaver exams.

In a perfect world at least, those students will not have to fight for opportunity or be subject to prejudice. Those that study hard will be rewarded. This is a very positive thing in many ways but it also has its drawbacks. Although school aims to be as a fair and as equal as possible, the real world is not always like that and life after school can sometimes come as a shock. The real world is a big and potentially scary place. Cultures, languages, climates and customs all differ and even within your own culture people can have very different outlooks and attitudes. In most western and capitalist societies, there is a complex and competitive nature which means that each member must pursue their own ambitions rather than expect society to provide them with a smooth and simple path to their goals.

Sport and Formula 1 are all about competition and winning. They are not fair or equal by their very nature. This notion applies not only on the racetrack but also inside the teams and in day to day experience within the job roles of F1. To make progress you must go out and make opportunities for yourself. The road to a career in motorsport is not mapped out for you in a structured way like school and formal education is. A job in Formula 1 is not awarded to the top students automatically or based on how enthusiastic they may be about the sport. Those who make it in this sport are typically those who have gone out and forged relationships, gathered experience and knowledge that others have missed.

F1 is a competitive business. It's a sport and nobody takes part unless they want to win. It is also about invention and original thought. The sport is constantly evolving and the technologies that make the difference between winning and losing are always changing too. It's a real cliché but in Formula 1 if you stand still then you will go backwards and so to survive you must forge ahead at all times.

Why do life skills matter then? They matter because life in Formula 1 is competitive from the top to the bottom, both on the racetrack and at the factory. Winning does not come easily, no matter how much money you have and however easy it looks on television. Winning comes through striving, grafting and thinking outside of the box, out of the ordinary. The best people in F1 see a way of improving an already amazing machine, a way of winning where the second place and also-rans do not. To be really successful in Formula 1 you need to find your own way, make things happen and not wait to be told or shown what to do.

Earlier in this book we talked about the personal skills and attributes that

Formula 1 teams need from their employees such as self-motivation, persistence, and will power to go the extra mile. If you pick up an average CV or resume you will see these kinds of words repeated quite regularly because they are very easy to say but they are very hard to demonstrate. When we recruit someone into a Formula 1 team we want to know that this person can push themselves without supervision, that they will work through difficult problems to a resolution without someone having to guide them and will not let down the team when they are needed most. There are many intelligent people in the world but these good character traits are far more rare.

Formula 1 is a high pressure environment. Be in no doubt that it is difficult. I have worked in motorsport for nearly 2 decades and have gathered a great deal of experience in that arena but I still find it tough. Even inside the teams that are winning there will be deadlines, reliability problems, money pressures, equipment failures or development projects that ask the impossible. It can often seem that there is no way through it and you will need to draw on your personal strength to keep motivated. You are competing against your counterparts in similar roles in the other teams so unless you dig deep, put in maximum effort and use the life skills that you have to drive forward your project then you will lose the battle. F1 teams need people who have that drive to want to win and push through. If you are someone who needs to be told what to do, when to do it and walk away when the going gets tough then perhaps motorsport is not for you.

In many ways, the process of getting a job in F1 is a test to see how resourceful, how determined and how creative you can be. The fact that it is not simply a case of going to school and then applying for a job could act to filter out those who want the easy route and are not sufficiently motivated to go the extra mile to fulfil their goal. As I said earlier, F1 is a competitive sport all the way from the racetrack down to even getting a job and so you should prepare for that by testing yourself in difficult situations and developing the skills to overcome them. This book is just a little helping hand to point you in the right direction.

Compared to many industries, Formula 1 teams get a high volume of applicants for each vacancy that they advertise. This is especially true when advertising for graduate, junior or work placement positions. Many of the applications are purely speculative in that the candidates have no real idea what the job entails or what qualifications they need. Of the credible applications that we get I am always amazed to see just how similar the vast majority of those applications are. We get applications from a lot of very good students, who have very high grades and clearly study hard but what makes recruiting so difficult is how to separate those people out between the "good" and the "exceptional". As an F1 team we want the best people we can get and normally it is the things that you do outside of school that make the difference and allow us to separate out the winning candidates.

Looking at most applications, 75% of them will be near identical. This majority will follow a very fixed formula, simply listing school grades, a choice of university perhaps with a good degree and then list a range of skills such as knowledge of computer programs like Microsoft Office and perhaps a CAD system they have used in their studies. A proportion may also include their participation in a Formula Student team, describing how they carried out such and such a role and attended their national Formula Student event at the end of the year.

Many of these students or applicants are of a good standard. Judged against the average man or woman in the street they will be very well suited for a role in an engineering firm. What makes it difficult for F1 teams is that there are so many applicants of similar or identical standard that it makes it difficult to select one over another. I don't wish to put down people's achievements but I must be brutally honest here when I say that my job becomes a little frustrating when you see the 30th near identical application that you have read that day. The school might be different and one person may have a slightly higher grade in their second year at university than another and on balance they are all very good but they are all very similar. There is little to make them stand out from the crowd.

The truth is that there are lots of good people out there who want to work in F1 and you need to be different. You need break out of this mould if you want to give yourself the maximum chance of working in F1. Being satisfied with "good" isn't good enough. As I said earlier in this section, the general education that you need to get into F1 is very fixed, very standard and you should not deviate from that but a general education alone will leave you lost in the crowd.

It's a real pleasure when I get a CV with something different on it. Reading job applications can be quite dull but presented with an interesting CV with some original experiences written by someone who has forged their own opportunities in life can be very refreshing. I would estimate that I spend only 1 to 2 minutes reading most job applications which isn't long. I will normally only look at the degree mark, University, A-Level grades and then skim read the initial section on work experience or out of school activities. If nothing catches my eye, that application goes into the "no good" pile and I move on. That doesn't give you very long to impress and I would imagine that most F1 recruiters do the same. Until you have a work history in motorsport or a similar industry then your activities in your personal time will be your only chance to impress. It is up to you to go out and make the most of the opportunities that are there and to get yourself to the top of the pile.

It's important to understand this concept of making opportunities before we go too much further so I wanted to pause on this point and just emphasise what I mean. Let me use two imaginary people as an example and to demonstrate the difference between waiting for opportunity and making opportunity.

"Joe" is a university student and has been a lifelong F1 fan. He watches every race, buys F1 magazines and has been to several Grand Prix as a spectator with his friends. He is determined to become an engineer in F1. He had exceptionally good grades at school and is top of his class studying Mechanical Engineering at a well regarded university. He has done all of the things that I recommended in the chapters on education and followed the path laid out for him. As he nears the end of his course and begins to think about his first job he looks at the websites of the F1 teams but does not see any graduate schemes or jobs on offer. He reads motorsport magazines but every job that is advertised there requires experience, which he does not have. He goes back each week to the same places but with no luck and so he is turned away believing that no jobs or opportunities exist in F1. There is no obvious way of progression from the steps he has made in education which will then lead him into his dream job in racing and he does not understand how this can be. Like many others in his situation he concludes that F1 is a closed door, open only to people who know others in the business and is somehow unfair or crooked.

To support himself with an income he gets a job at a large aerospace firm and settles into a very successful but frankly ordinary career. He never gets to fulfil his childhood dream of working at the Monaco Grand Prix. He often rues the corrupt world of motorsport for denying him his chance to work in racing which he feels he was more than capable of doing.

Our second imaginary person "Rich" on the other hand is a more average school student. He is not stupid but even though he works incredibly hard at school, he is not top of the class and struggles to shine. He too dreams of working in Formula 1 and watches every scrap of TV coverage during race weekends.

Walking home from school one day Rich notices a man assembling a go-kart in his garage. He stops but is too shy to ask to take a look and so goes home, but he is left intrigued by the kart and what the man was doing. During the following few weeks he walks by several more times until eventually he sees the man again and walks straight up to introduce himself. The man is more than happy to show him and Rich helps him with tools and assembling the floor tray and side pods of the kart. They strike up an immediate friendship, discussing racing and how much they enjoy it. Eventually Rich becomes Keith's trackside helper and accompanies him to several local races becoming familiar with basic tools, mechanics, kart setup and the way that race meetings are run. He gets a real taste for petrol fumes, tyre rubber and the buzz of competition.

At school, Rich uses his new found kart racing experience to focus a design and make project. Keith has been after a frame and measuring device that allows him to quickly setup his kart's track width and front toe setting and so Rich uses the school workshop to design and manufacture a lightweight folding frame that fits the bill perfectly. His work on the project also leads to one of his teachers revealing that a neighbour of theirs runs a small hill climb car and agrees to introduce them so that Rich can take a look. He again spends several long evenings helping prepare that car and travelling to race meetings. He develops a friendship with the owner and several other privateer racers in the series who give him advice and knowledge about the industry and who to talk to.

When Rich goes to university he applies for a bursary to help his studies and is granted the award based on his project work and experience in amateur racing. He uses this award and the industry knowledge he has gained from his contacts to apply for a work placement at Pilbeam hill climb cars in Lincolnshire and spends a year designing suspension components for high powered single seaters, working alongside several ex-Formula 1 designers and other staff. He travels to Snetterton circuit at the weekends and watches club races and several national single seater and touring car meetings dropping off his CV with team managers and talking to influential people.

When Rich nears the end of his degree and begins to think about a full time job he already has an offer on the table from Pilbeam irrespective of what his degree mark is but uses his already impressive CV to apply to several other race car manufacturers and lands a job at Prodrive in their rally trackside team as a junior data engineer. He travels to world rally championship events all over the globe and becomes proficient in damper setup and ride analysis on the rough gravel tracks and asphalt. Two years later a Formula 1 team advertises for a vehicle dynamicist with ride experience in top level motorsport. Rich was perfectly placed to apply and got the job. His career in F1 has begun and only 2 years out of university he already has a wide experience in racing and the opportunity to work at the industry's top level.

The examples may be (partly) fiction but they are very typical. I hope that you can see the differences in approach that the 2 people took even though they are from very similar backgrounds and arguably Joe was the more academically qualified of the two. He followed the school system and excelled but did not use his time to make contacts and gain experience. His life skills were not put to the test and he did not develop himself outside of school and so when his formal education finished he found himself with nowhere to go and with little or no understanding of the industry he so wanted to be a part of. To him Formula 1 looked like a closed door because he did not see the way in and so took his career elsewhere and resented those (like Rich) who appeared to have lucked in. I feel sorry for him in a way but he made mistakes and expected opportunities to be there for him instead of working towards creating his own opportunities. He did not have the necessary life skills and did not work hard enough away from the classroom.

Joe and people like him believe that F1 is unfair, excludes people and does not offer young people opportunities. Many of them are quite bitter about it too. You have probably heard people like him telling you how it is impossible to get into F1 and that you should not waste your time. He will probably also go on to tell you how hard people are worked, how little they get paid and how everybody who works in F1 hates it anyway. There are many of these people on the forums of popular motorsport websites but you'll find that not one of them has ever set foot inside a Formula 1 team factory never mind had a job there. Needless to say, you should ignore then.

Rich on the other hand started in the same place or even at a disadvantage but his natural curiosity and work ethic made him grab opportunities with both hands. Lending a helping hand to a hobbyist kart racer at a local track is a far cry from the glamorous world of Formula 1 but it is where so many successful drivers and engineers get their first taste of racing. It almost doesn't matter what form of racing or what kind of vehicle it is because the lessons, feelings and skills are all the same. Each opportunity he took taught him something new and opened up further opportunities down the line as he built his experience and credibility. With experience under his belt, even at the very lowest level he was taken seriously by others in the racing scene and set himself apart as someone who went out and took part in motorsport rather than simply watching it on television. By the time he finished his degree, he had a range of skills and experiences that were valued in a full time motorsport job. He had not raced himself nor had he spent a fortune taking part but he was accepted and recognised as a member of the racing community. Once his education was finished, he already knew where to look to find the next stage of his career and that ultimately led him to Formula 1 in just a few short years. Joe may say that Rich was lucky and perhaps he was in some ways but he put himself in those positions and was there ready for it when it came. As the great golfer Gary Player once said "the more I practice, the luckier I get" and that is never more true than in motorsport. In reality you make your own luck.

The mistakes that Joe made are unfortunately very common and are the primary reason why so many who wish to get a job in Formula 1 fail to do so. I do not want you to do the same. If you expect to go to school, get a degree and then apply to a Formula 1 team and immediately become a race engineer or designer then I'm afraid you will almost certainly be disappointed. The road to F1 is not a straight one but I hope this book can convince you that you do not need to be like Joe and that you can make a career in motorsport without money or privilege. This book was written to open your eyes and show you how to forge your own opportunities and fulfil your goals. I and many like me are testament that it can be done so hope I can convince you. The remaining chapters will guide you along the way and show you how to find opportunities where others fail to see them.

5 Get out, get involved, get in

In the previous chapter, we discussed why it is so important to make the most of every opportunity that you get and to build on your experiences one by one.

It's very easy to say how determined, resourceful, and hard working you are but to make your mark you need to be able to PROVE it. Actions will speak much louder than words in this case and so there really is no substitute for getting out there and doing it. We saw in the previous chapter how two very similar individuals, Joe and Rich, ended up in very different careers despite them both being very capable people. Joe followed a very straight road in front of him and concentrated only on his school work whereas Rich built up a range of experiences in motorsport by taking every opportunity that he got and learning through the advice and guidance of people that he met on the way. In Rich's case, he was able to get involved in some grass roots motorsport and see first hand how race events are run, feel the pressure of a big event and see how important it is to be properly prepared and organised. It may not have been Formula 1 but the lessons are the same up and down the racing ladder. These are the things that school cannot teach you.

As I mentioned earlier I am not a big believer in luck but you might say that luck played a part in Rich's experiences. Not everyone knows somebody who races or lives close enough to a racetrack to make it practical to go and watch at weekends. Making that first step is often the most difficult but in fact it does not really matter what you do with your time, only that you got out there and did it. If you can prove that you can make things happen in one arena then you will have proven that you can make things happen in any arena and this is the attribute of most value.

Not many of you will live across the road from Brands Hatch or on the same street as a successful Formula 3 team. If only life were that simple. I grew up in a part of the UK well outside of the motorsport valley region where most of the race teams and suppliers in my country are based. That does not however mean that there are not activities near you that you can join in with. You must work with the cards that you are dealt but in the age of the internet you should be able to conduct simple research to find out what motorsport activities are going on in your region. It may not be Formula 1 but you may be surprised how much there is.

A good starting point is the RACMSA which is the governing body of all sanctioned motorsport in the UK. Almost every country in the world will have a similar governing body which is affiliated to the Federation Internationale de l'Automobile (FIA) which governs the majority of international motorsport series including Formula 1.

http://www.fia.com/about-fia/member-clubs

From here you can find regional organisers and member clubs who arrange race meetings and series from the very grass roots of the sport to national championships. It is highly likely that there is something going on near you that will interest you. The variety of motorsports is quite staggering and extends far beyond just circuit racing.

https://www.msauk.org/The-Sport/Types-of-Motor-Sport

In the UK and most other countries, motorsports events are supported and marshalled by an enthusiastic army of volunteers and you can become a marshal from the age of 11 (not trackside until age 16). You will see these heroes of racing at almost every event dressed in their bright orange outfits waving flags and retrieving crashed or broken cars. Even for the F1 Grand Prix at Silverstone the marshals are volunteers who do it for the love of racing. Their seats for the race are as close to the action as you can get and are a viewpoint that money cannot buy.

https://www.msauk.org/Get-Started/Volunteering

Getting involved in racing in this way will not only get you free entry to race meetings but it will get you into a racing community where you can begin to learn from others and make contacts in the same way that Rich did in my earlier example. Organisers are almost always short of help and so it should not be difficult to make yourself useful.

Many marshals will race themselves or will have done so in the past so more than likely you will be able to find somebody who you get on with who can show you what a racing car looks like and perhaps even enlist your help in preparing it. As we have seen, they key is that once you are into the community you can build your contacts and make further opportunities from them.

Some great events to get involved with are at local kart races as these are much more widespread across the country than full race circuits. If you are under the age of 16 you are also much more likely to meet people of your own age as kids can start kart racing from the age of 8 in the UK. National clubs can be found at:

http://www.abkc.org.uk/clubs/

If you are serious about getting involved in either grass roots or professional car preparation you can start to contact owners and teams directly. Cold calling will never have the same success rate as personal introduction but if you can find somebody local to you it may be possible simply to ask to meet with them and take a look at their car at a race meeting and potentially offer some help or support. Many people will be in need of the potential help but care should be taken about how you make your approach as every racer will have invested time and money into their project and are unlikely to share it with total strangers. Invest your time in getting to know someone before asking too much.

Most series organisers will have entrant lists with contact details or may know someone who needs help who they can put you in touch with. If you don't ask, you don't get. For example, this is the entrant list for the British MSA Formula (Formula Ford) series.

http://www.britishformulaford.co.uk/series-info/teams-list/

The process of building up slowly may also be a good thing to bear in mind at this point. If you make an approach to a lower Formula team, even on a voluntary basis, think about how much more credible you will appear if you have spent a season organising dummy grids at your local kart track or even directing traffic at a hill climb meeting. Each experience builds on the last and you need to inch your way along. That is exactly what Rich did in our earlier example and it really works.

Remember too that racing takes place on two wheels as well as four so cast your net as wide as you can even if F1 is your ultimate goal.

http://en.m.wikipedia.org/wiki/Motorcycle_racing

http://www.acu.org.uk/Centres-Clubs/

When I talk to people about volunteering in motorsport and working for free to build up experience they often look at me like I am slightly insane. Working for free seems like a strange concept. It is easy to assume that money is plentiful throughout motorsport. The facts are that most motorsports would not happen if it wasn't for volunteers and by that I am not just talking about the marshals and lap counters. In club racing, almost all mechanics and pit crew will be family, friends or volunteers who do it for the love of it rather than any financial gain. Many work in professional racing during the week and help with amateur racing at weekends. So common is this type of volunteer that they have their own name - weekend warrior.

A weekend warrior is the description applied to anyone who works in motorsport voluntarily on their weekends and during their free time. They are the backbone of racing and you will find them at any race circuit at almost any time from karting to semi- professional single seaters. You would be well advised to try and join them.

Several websites have popped up which are dedicated to uniting willing volunteers and competitors in need of spare hands and so even if you can't get to meet drivers in person then you might find some useful leads via these sites.

http://www.racedaystaff.com

http://www.myweekendwarrior.com

Don't look at it as working for free. You must view it as a fantastic opportunity to gain experience and boost your CV. The benefits are mutual and can lead to some professional opportunities down the road especially if you make friends and contacts. Make the most of it.

It's so easy to think that the people who take part in motorsport are rich kids who have the world at their feet. That is very rarely the case. At club level in particular, most competitors are cash strapped and struggle for the time to run their racing as well as they would like. A helping hand is so very welcome for these people and it is in fact very easy for you to be of assistance to many of them. This applies even to professional racing. I know a student who was a data engineer at Le Mans in his spare time simply through volunteering. When I saw his CV I wanted to speak to him straightaway.

I have also heard of aspiring marketing or motorsport journalists approaching club or low level single seater racers and offering to produce marketing and PR material for them. Very often it is more than enough just to prepare a car and run it at the circuit that people at this level can barely consider promotional material or sponsorship campaigns to help fund their racing. Agencies are prohibitively expensive on their budgets.

If an able young man or woman comes to them and offers these kinds of services then they are very likely to not only be interested but to bite your hand off. Many of them are likely to jump at the chance and will be happy for you to produce a website, some promotional material or call round local companies and suppliers on their behalf. One of the best things is that you can do this type work at arm's length, especially now with the popularity of the internet so even location is no barrier. You will see first-hand what racing promotion is all about and get to learn some real-world skills with no risk or commitment on your behalf. You might even strike up some relationships or contacts that can be of use in your real career later. Use your imagination but the opportunities are there in abundance so what have you got to lose?

Ideally you will be able to build up some experience and knowledge of real motorsport alongside your studies. Motorsport is after all why we are here. If that really is not possible you should still consider getting involved in another form of sport or a competitive organisation which has close parallels to racing. Often, the very fact that you went out and did *something* rather than nothing is what will catch the eye of recruiters.

Personal sports such as running, triathlon, swimming or cycling share many of the driven goals and motivations that motorsport requires and is valuable way to demonstrate that you can push to a difficult goal. I am not talking here about doing a one off 5K run in your local park however, that may not impress, but a consistent regime of training towards a far off goal like a marathon, a swimming time trial or cycle tour through the alps will demonstrate the driven side of your personality. Many people who work in F1 have these hobbies outside of the office.

Creating your own event on any scale requires a level of organisation and drive and can be something that might set you apart from the crowd. That event might be a social event at school or university such as an end of year sports day, a class reunion or industrial trips to local companies. I have heard of individuals arranging factory tours at local racing teams or circuits for class mates which probably required some impressive talking but this would be just the thing if you were aiming to get into the marketing side of the sport. A key skill is persuading somebody that they can benefit from what you want to do.

Societies are very popular at most universities and organising positions within those societies are always good material for a CV or resume. I have heard of individuals creating entirely new societies to fit their own interests and generating funding to run them which is highly impressive but be wary that it needs to suit a wider audience not just yourself. Why not combine two examples above and create an industrial visit society? If you can back it with the name of the university and some positive careers publicity for the companies involved then maybe you will have a better chance? Thinking of your own ideas always gets credit well above following the crowd.

Entrepreneurship of any sort is also a very valuable skill and if you have invented, created or sold something that creates a small business then shout about it on your resume. I had an application at one time from a student who serviced and repaired bikes for fellow students in his hall of residence. Not only did he earn valuable funds for student life but he vastly increased his mechanical skills and built up a collection of tools and parts that he could use for his own projects in the future. I've also seen someone who created websites for kart racers and junior race drivers, undercutting professional firms and gaining valuable contacts in the process.

Dealing with people and the ability to make things happen against the tide are the key skills here and whatever you want to do or have the opportunity to do can be credit worthy if you see it through. If it was easy, you can't expect much credit but whatever it is just get out there and start doing it because you never know who you will meet, what you can learn and what it may lead to next. As the next section will tell you, success is all about stepping stones and identifying open doors that others fail to see.

Part 5 : The real secrets to a career in Formula 1

1 There is no secret

I have spoken to and discussed the subject of a career in F1 with many people and I'm often put on the spot and asked to say what I think the secret to working in F1 is. I think many people expect a reply with a one line answer containing some revealing secret or solution which can magically open a motorsport career to anyone who wants it. I honestly wish I could do that but as you might well have guessed already, I simply can't. Life is not that simple. Short of granting each person a job at my own team (and I wouldn't last long in my position if I did that) I don't have a simple answer for them.

The fact that those people assume that there is a magic ingredient to the whole industry also reveals that they probably believe that the sport is governed by rules or run by some kind of secret club or society. This society must be one which decides to only let in people who have contacts or the right connections. It's easy to assume that someone or something controls who gets in and who does not but I can assure you that there is no such society or control.

We have already seen how frustration can lead to a myth such as this being repeated and spread as fact but believe me it is 100% untrue. I hope this book can dispel such myths and show you the real and honest way to get into the sport. This chapter examines why these rumours start and how by ignoring them you can put yourself in an even stronger position to capitalise over those who are gullible enough to believe in them.

F1 often appears to be a bit of a mystery, a closed door and a separate world to those on the outside. The sport's technology is a heavily guarded secret because of the intense competition between the rival teams but that secretive atmosphere tends to be applied to many other aspects of the industry even if it is not intentional. Traditionally F1 teams have not needed to supply a great deal of career advice to potential employees because the sport's popularity has meant a plentiful supply of well qualified people have been falling over themselves to compete for jobs. The reality is that most teams get so many speculative letters and applications from fans that the last thing they want to do is encourage more. Many of those applying ask to be just given the chance to prove themselves which in an ideal world they would be, but when the numbers spread to hundreds or thousands then there is simply no way that a team could do that and still function as a race team. It takes a great deal of time and money to invest in new blood and so how would you decide who was worthy of the chance and who was not?

Filtering good applicants from the bad is a real problem, especially when those people are totally new to the business. Enthusiastic newcomers do not always know what they are getting themselves into and even if they are well qualified their personalities may not be suited to working in a racing team. As a result, the teams are reluctant to open their doors too easily and prefer to use work placements or recruit from other racing companies to filter out the good from the bad.

This closed door appearance is where the problem and the misinformation starts. The truth is that F1 teams are very interested in nurturing and developing young talent but experience has shown them that many would be employees are more interested in hanging around the paddock and mixing with movie stars than in developing racing cars. The reality of life in a Formula 1 team is sometimes quite different to how some may imagine it and it is only when the hard work starts that a team can really discover whether a new recruit has what it takes or not. Teams cannot afford to carry people who are only along for the ride so they hesitate to take risks. This reluctance to take a chance on unfamiliar newcomers is generally what is interpreted as the closed door and secret society.

I know when I was in my teens I looked up to those who worked in the sport tremendously but the paddock gates seemed like an impenetrable barrier to a life that I didn't understand and I wasn't a part if. I used to ask myself "What do these people know and what have they done to become part of this untouchable world?" The distance between myself and them seemed vast and so alien that I could not see a way to cross that huge divide. There seemed no logical solution.

As many of you will be in the same position that I was back then, it is easy to assume that to unlock the gate you require some secret knowledge or unwritten rule which only a privileged few have the answer to. It is easy to assume that there must be some a secret or that you need to know an insider to get you in. As more people experience this frustration and talk about it with others so the myth gathers pace and soon it becomes "fact". People who believe in the myths will be very happy to tell you that Formula 1 teams do not take on school leavers or graduates and that you cannot get a job in F1 no matter how hard you try. They will tell you that it is because you are not part of the secret society or did not go to the right university.

Let's take a step backwards for a second and look at the facts. It should be clear that F1 teams do in fact recruit young people and nurture their developing talent. Any company which intends to stay in business for the long term needs to do this to grow or to replace its more experienced staff that leave or retire. With the pace of development in F1 we need to do this simply to survive. To pass up the opportunity to recruit new and talented people would be competitive suicide and so we are always on the lookout.

F1 is in fact a very young sport. If you look at the guys and girls of any pit crew up and down the pitlane you will see that the average age is somewhere around the late 20's. Motorsport is an industry where you can learn very quickly and many senior staff are significantly younger their equivalents in "normal" industries. The energy required by this career lends itself to young people and you will see many youthful faces emerging from the reception doors at F1 factories around the world. The question is therefore where do these new people come from if the factory doors are closed to the majority who go seeking employment in F1? I hope I can show you in the chapters that follow that the answer is quite simple.

I could use a cliché and say that the only secret to working in F1 is hard work. Whilst that is true to an extent, I know that this hard work needs to be directed in a particular way to get maximum effect. Hard work alone will not help you if it is misdirected, especially by bad advice from people who do not know what they are talking about.

I thankfully never fell into the trap of believing in secrets or privilege when it came to my career. Perhaps that was naivety on my part but I simply refused to accept that this career was meant to be for someone else and not for me. If I tried to imagine myself as an accountant or a teacher whilst somebody else got to travel the world and design Formula 1 cars I honestly felt a near physical pain. I could not accept it and refused to listen to anyone who tried to convince me otherwise. My parents and my teachers all tried to convince me that F1 was too narrow and too specialist to expect to get a job there and that I would be better suited to a more normal career. I was wasting my time they told me.

I knew deep down however that the engineers and mechanics on the other side of the paddock gate were just normal everyday people. They had to be. If that was the case then that there was no good reason why I could not be one of them. I was not interested in a normal career and was not about to listen to anybody who spoke without knowledge of motorsport and what it took to get there. I decided to get out there and learn for myself and I am so very glad that I did. I did not believe in secrets and neither should you.

I recently spoke with a young university student who had read about a scheme which was being promoted by the Williams F1 team and Autosport magazine. It offered the chance of a 2-year graduate scheme at the Williams F1 factory including trackside experience to the successful candidate. A selection of universities had agreed to take part in the scheme and would nominate their most promising student to the judging panel based on their academic record but also on their enthusiasm and motivation for a career in racing. The student that I spoke with did not attend any of the universities who were taking part in the scheme and was therefore not eligible for that award.

He was understandably disappointed by this but instead of regrouping his efforts to pursue an F1 career via another route he declared to me that he was giving up his dream there and then. His rationale was that there was clearly a pre-agreed secret or club between the teams and the universities who were involved in the Williams award scheme. He thought that anybody who went to the university that he attended was excluded from working in motorsport *entirely*. He honestly believed that no matter how hard he worked, it was already written that he was not allowed to have a career in racing because he had not attended the right university. He believed that because of the scheme announced by Williams, he had found the secret to a career in F1 but had found it too late and was now as a result excluded.

I must say I was very disappointed when I heard this. The experience was clearly difficult for him but his actions contradicted all the facts that he had before him because he had allowed the myths and doubts to cloud his judgement. He had fallen into the trap of believing in secrets and had used this as an excuse to allow himself to give up.

It's much easier to walk away from something difficult when you believe that there is a conspiracy against you or that you are excluded from something for reasons out of your control. If you believe that someone has already decided your destiny for you then it is easy to use that belief to explain to others why you have not achieved what you set out to achieve. The notion of a secret to working in F1 is very easy to use as an excuse for giving up.

The truth is that for this student, the disappointment should only have hardened his resolve to succeed, not destroy it. The Williams scheme sounds very lucrative and I am sure that somebody somewhere will benefit from it and potentially start a successful career but it is one job amongst hundreds or even thousands in the motorsport industry. I don't know anyone who made their career through such a scheme and it should be obvious that this one is almost entirely about marketing and publicity for the Williams team and for Autosport magazine. It's a great idea but let's face it, it is as much about the team and the other institutions involved as it is about the students. This is an artificial situation created by marketing people, it is not reality.

I was disheartened to see that one disappointment could end the hopes of an individual like that and I very much hope that he will recover and try again. The idea of the secret to F1 lurks in many people's minds and is always there to fall back on as a reason to give up but there really is no reason to at all. The fact that so many do however should only strengthen your resolve because if you can stay motivated and follow the guidance in this book then you will be one of the ones that makes it. It is not as difficult as it appears and I hope to show you a clear path over the next few chapters.

Whilst there is no single secret to a career in F1, the very purpose of this book is to shed some light on how best to go about making a career in racing. Nothing that I share with you in this book is a secret but I hope that what I can do is to reassure you that a job in F1 is not out of reach, that it is normal, achievable and realistic for anyone who wants to dedicate themselves to it.

The fact that there is no secret path or club in F1 is great news for you and everyone else. It means that you can make a career in F1 from any background, university or country in the world. If you offer skills and attitude that a team may value they will not care where you come from. All they care about is winning. F1 teams are always looking for new ideas and new technologies and so if you come to them from a new or diverse background and can convince them that you have something to offer then they will take notice. The fact that there is no single accepted path, route or rule into F1 should encourage you and I hope you see it as great news.

My own background has nothing to do with racing whatsoever. Of my wider family, I am the only one who works in racing and my parents, siblings, aunties and uncles have no interest or knowledge of the industry at all. Many of them keep an eye on results now as they know that I am involved but some would still be unsure of which team I worked for. I am probably one of those people that you would consider an outsider or someone without a privileged background yet here I am doing the job I dreamt of.

Racing is something I learnt about the hard way, worked my way into and got to know over time and you should be doing the same. I didn't discover any single secret on my way but I also found racing a very open and welcoming community when approached in the right way. F1's popularity means that the main doors may be closed upon first glance but if you look beyond then you will see that racing is a very open and welcoming sport. The doors are there if you are prepared to look hard enough and you don't need any secrets to open them.

The following chapters describe the ways in which most people who work in F1 got to be where they are and none of it is particularly secretive or clever. It simply requires a little bit of knowledge and research beyond the edges of F1.

2 Work placements and apprenticeships

In the previous chapter, we discussed how F1 is a sport which nurtures and develops young talent. This claim often surprises people as there are rarely any advertisements for jobs in Formula 1 teams which do not require prior experience. It is hard to see how these young people are given the chance to start their career.

As we know, F1 requires a certain work ethic, attitude and personality that it is very hard to judge in someone's character without getting to know them first. Paper applications and even interviews in person can be misleading and so F1 teams ideally want to get to know people before they commit to offering them a permanent job. Advertising for newcomers is a risky business and teams are understandably reluctant to take the chance. F1 teams are still relatively small businesses and so even just a few poor recruits can have a big impact.

Work placements and apprenticeships however offer the teams a different way to recruit. They give teams the chance to take a much longer look at how individuals fit into the team and how they develop themselves in a real working environment. Work placements are normally only for a defined period of a few months or a year and so there is no commitment for a team to take things any further if an individual does not fit in the team well or shows poor attitude. The teams use these placements as one of their primary sources of new talent and so they offer the aspiring F1 employee a golden opportunity.

The most difficult hurdle to forging a career in Formula 1 is getting that elusive first F1 job, that breakthrough step into the apparently closed world of professional motorsport. In this chapter, I'll describe why work placements are one of the best opportunities to get your foot in the door, where to find them and how to make the most of them if you are lucky enough to be chosen.

For university students, predominantly those people studying engineering but also for management and marketing students, the single most likely way to break into the sport straight from studying these days is through work placements. Almost all the current F1 teams take on undergraduates on long placement programmes (normally a full 12 months or more) and this is for several reasons:

- Students are a source of relatively cheap labour
- The programme allows a team to develop relationships with universities for research purposes
- Student placements are lower risk than a graduate recruitment programme

The first two in that list are genuine plus points for the teams but it is really the last and final point that is the most relevant for those wishing to break into the sport. I am often asked where graduate vacancies are advertised, or where those jobs are that say No experience necessary. Bad news really, they are few and far between. We've mentioned risk already and taking on inexperienced people carries very significant risk.

Imagine a team wants to take on a graduate, or perhaps several. They might post an advert on autosport.com or on racestaff.com and receive hundreds of applications from interested people. Firstly, they will have the non-trivial task of sorting through those hundreds of applications and selecting the 5 or 10 resumes that look promising. As so many of the applications will look so similar this is something of a lottery.

They then must invite each person for an interview and they then have just an hour or so to find out everything about those people and decide whether they have a future with that team and make them a committed offer. It's a very difficult process (have you ever considered what it is like to be on the opposite side of the table during an interview?) and carries enormous risk. I was involved in choosing a new graduate at a previous team and the candidate we chose performed very well in the interview but was lazy, over- confident and a poor engineer when it came to working full time. It was a big mistake which we could not undo easily.

The biggest advantage of a work placement scheme for an F1 team is that they get to see potential recruits working and developing their skills in the right environment over a reasonable period of time. It is in effect a 12-month long job interview and it's normally clear to the team after that period which candidates will make good F1 engineers and which will not. The students who are not suitable will go back to university to finish their degree and will probably not hear from the team again. Those who performed well however are likely to be invited back to take up a full-time job once their studies have been completed. The job will probably not be advertised on the website or in the press but it does exist. This is the magic, or unseen graduate recruitment process in F1 and why the places are seldom or never advertised. Some teams do still recruit graduates fresh from university but this is the exception rather than the rule. For university or school level people, work placements are as good an opportunity as you are going to get. You should *not* let it slip.

Do as much homework on work placements as you possibly can by contacting the teams early and asking for details of their program. They may not publicise it a great deal in order to limit the number of applicants so it is up to you to get out there and find out about it. Leaving it until immediately before your placement year begins is much too late and will be a clear sign to the teams that you are not organised and not a serious candidate. Your competition will be prepared and you risk being left behind.

Several teams invite applications from September for placements which begin in July of the following year and will carry out the full selection process before Christmas. Don't wait until the summer holidays are approaching because the door will have firmly shut. That will be your fault and nobody else's.

The following text is taken directly from an advert on the Williams F1 website.

As part of Williams' ongoing commitment to support Universities in supplying the talented engineers to the Formula One industry in the future, we operate a 12-month student placement programme.

Student Placement Opportunities Available

The Company receives many applications from students who would like the opportunity to undertake student placements. Due to such high demand, along with limited availability due to our company size, resources and racing commitments we are only able to accommodate the following opportunities each year:

Maximum of 10 paid student one year placements

Students will work under the mentorship of an experienced team member, gaining significant experience, as well as invaluable information for final year dissertations / thesis. Along the way students will pick up a diverse range of new skills and competencies that can be universally applied in an environment that is constantly changing.

Throughout the duration of the placement, the student will have regular performance evaluations with the nominated manager to aid professional and personal development. The Company's informal working culture will also allow the student to network with the full spectrum of people working within the team.

Only students taking part in the student placement programmes can be accommodated in our Aerodynamics, Design and Test Facilities Departments.

RICHARD LADBROOKE

We do not offer student placement opportunities on our Race or Test Teams.

Student Placement Application Process

When shortlisting student placement applications the Company generally expects students to be studying relevant subjects at university in subjects such as Mechanical Design and Aeronautical Design and have a minimum of two years experience at University before the placement starts. It is also essential that you should return to your course for a minimum of one year following completion of the placement. We are unable to accept applications from students in their final year of university studies.

In addition to the above, active participation in programmes such as Formula Student, F1 in schools may be an advantage as well as demonstrating an active interest in leisure activities such as go-karting, restoring or working on cars, building working models of cars and planes.

When applying for student placements opportunities, all students are expected to submit a covering letter along with a curriculum vitae containing the following information:

- *Your current career aims and how you plan to achieve them*
- *Subjects that you are currently taking and plan to take*
- *Relevant leisure pursuits and activities*
- *Why work experience with the Company would be beneficial to you*
- *Demonstrate that you are the best person to be selected*

Applications

Applications for the student placement programmes should be uploaded through our website by visiting www.williamsf1.com. Your application will be acknowledged within two weeks of you sending us the application. We will not accept applications which are not submitted through our website, any paper-based applications will be returned to the sender with a copy of this policy.

Too good to be true?

When I was at school and even when I studied at University, opportunities like this barely existed. I wrote to every team asking about a work placement but without success. The industry was too small for that at the time (or maybe I wasn't good enough, I don't know). To have such an ordered and structured programme advertised with such a large number of placements available is a golden opportunity. This is exactly the kind of opening that you need to be ready for.

We've already seen that you need to be considering and researching work placement schemes as early as you possibly can to avoid missing the deadlines for applications. You'll notice too how much Williams have emphasised the need to detail your *relevant* hobbies and interests outside of study and how an advantage can be gained by demonstrating involvement in practical engineering and racing outside of school and university. It is a competition for places and you need to throw as much at it as you possibly can.

I hope it is obvious to you that the best people will have been gaining those experiences and participating in those relevant activities for many years prior to the time they apply for a work placement. You will be making life very hard for yourself if you wait until somebody asks you to demonstrate your relevant experience before you go out and try and get it. My chapter on getting out and getting involved was all about this and I hope now you see why it was so important. Don't wait, because if you do then someone else will already be out there doing it and they will be the one who gets the work placement instead of you. I think everyone would rather be following the example that Rich set as opposed to Joe in the comparison of the two students in my previous chapter.

Apprenticeship programmes are opportunities for school leavers or older candidates who are not in work or full time education to learn a trade or skill whilst earning a wage. Apprenticeships combine practical training in a real job with formal outside study on a related course or subject.

You will have the opportunity to learn not only from books and study but to work alongside experienced and skilled colleagues and learn in exactly the environment you hope then to be working full time. Apprenticeships last between 1 and 4 years depending on the placement.

Apprenticeships were very common in the UK in the 60's and 70's but fell out of favour when policy encouraged more and more students to attend university. They have seen something of a resurgence in recent years and now offer a much quicker and more relevant path to full time work for people who are not interested in university. This is particularly true in the STEM sector and most Formula 1 teams offer them for much the same reasons as I explained above. They offer the teams a chance to get to know an individual and watch them develop. A full-time job is not guaranteed at the end of the apprenticeship but I believe that nationally 85% of apprentices who complete the full period will then go onto a permanent and full time position.

In Formula 1 apprentices get involved at the very heart of what the team does from the very start. It is possible for an apprentice to attend races as part of the race team crew and to move around the factory in various roles and departments. As an opportunity to learn it is second to none and is a golden opportunity to launch a motorsport career if you see yourself in a more practical role.

Mercedes AMG High Performance Powertrains offer numerous apprenticeships each year and their website (as of December 2014) shows the following:

Our Advanced Apprenticeship programme provides the foundations for your career at Mercedes AMG High Performance Powertrains. We want talented, intelligent, enthusiastic people to join our world class engineering team.

In partnership with SEMTA, we offer you the training, guidance and support needed to complete an Advanced Apprenticeship over a 3-year period, based in our state of the art Technology Centre in Brixworth, Northamptonshire.

You will start on a salary of £14,000 that will rise to £19,000 towards the end of your apprenticeship. Additional benefits include an annual personal performance bonus, podium bonus (based on F1 race results), private healthcare, 36 days holiday (inclusive of Bank Holidays) and a 10% non-contributory pension.

We offer three kinds of Advanced Apprenticeships for you to choose from:

Apprentice Machinist We've invested in the latest machinery and we want you to learn how to manufacture complex components to the finest tolerances, for our Formula 1 powertrains. You'll develop skills in CNC machining, milling, grinding, turning, programming and other manufacturing processes

Apprentice Assembly Technician You'll learn how to assemble some of the most complicated cutting edge automotive technology to the highest possible standards ensuring every last component fits together perfectly. This will involve both mechanical and electrical components, giving you a breadth of experience and ensuring you have the versatility to work with future technological advances.

Test Operations Technician Working with a team of technicians and engineers you will learn to configure and run complex tests of both components and full F1 race engines in our state of the art testing facilities.

More details can be found at

https://careers.mercedes-amg-hpp.com

or on the websites of most of the other F1 teams.

General info for UK apprenticeships can be found at
https://www.gov.uk/further-education- skills/apprenticeships

F1 teams will not necessarily advertise their work placement programs in the wider press. Finding the details might require a little more research than normal but this can be one of the best ways to filter out those who are not serious candidates. Only those individuals who are determined to get to F1 will be pro-active enough to go looking and so it acts as an effective filter to reduce the human resources workload. Perhaps they will miss out on some very talented engineers or candidates but perseverance and going the extra mile is one of the core skills for anyone working in motorsport and so it's an effective first test. It is not difficult to read a website or even to cold call the human resources departments for details, persist if they do not answer at first.

Research can be a big source of help and information at this stage too. In the age of social media and online personality I would expect that most F1 work placement students and apprentices will brag about it to their friends or anyone else who wants to listen or read. I've seen and read quite a few such profiles and you can search Twitter for certain phrases and comments to help you find people who have been there. They will be more than happy to advise you I am sure if you get in touch. The link below should aid you in finding those relevant people.

https://support.twitter.com/articles/132700-using-twitter-search

LinkedIn can also be a valuable resource to find current apprentices or work placement students as their profiles will almost always detail their position and company. You can connect with them very easily as most people are keen to collect contacts and then you can ask them directly how they applied, where they studied, what the interview was like and what the name of their supervisor was. The connected nature of LinkedIn means that once you have found one placement student you will probably find them all as they will have connected with their colleagues and even the previous year's intake as they often overlap for a few months in the summer. The information and networking is there just waiting for you to find it. Find out more about how to do this at:

http://jobinf1.com/2013/10/11/research-your-way-into-formula-1-using-linkedin/

You can find all the websites and contact details for each Formula 1 team in the resources section at the end of this book.

Even if you are lucky enough to have been selected for your work placement, the battle is not yet won. As I suggested, a work placement is really a 12-month long job interview and you should treat it as such. It should not just be about those 12 months but you should see it as the opportunity to start a permanent career in racing. Here are some of my tips for making the most of it.

There is nothing worse than a student or school leaver who believes that they know everything about Formula 1. The real business is rather different to that which you see on TV so do not expect to be an expert in F1 just because you read magazines and watch television. You will not be expected to have detailed knowledge of what makes a car fast and what doesn't. You are there to learn, not to teach so stay humble.

First impressions last and it's important to get off to a good start. When you start your placement, it is likely to be the start of the main car design phase and many engineers will be working late to keep on top of the mounting workload. WORK HARD. I don't mean just for the sake of it or until the dead of night but show willing from the outset and work as hard as you can on whatever you are tasked with. You are likely to have been given access to the main drawing store with all the 3D models of the components which make up the car. Use that and learn for yourself even if you have finished what you are doing. Ask questions and absorb as much as you can. If you put your coat on and leave the moment that 5pm rolls around you are not likely to come across as a hard worker or a team player. You do not need to do this every day or for the whole year but if you make this enthusiastic start then you will give an immediately good impression.

It's important to ask questions and learn as much as you can. Your immediate manager is likely to be a source of vast knowledge for you and so not only will asking questions bring you greater understanding but it creates a good impression for those who will be deciding if you come back to work at the team permanently. Most Formula 1 teams have a flat structure in that everyone knows everyone and the team principal is often on first name terms with the cleaners and everyone in between. As a work placement student however you should not expect to sit and have a coffee with Adrian Newey or knock on his door for a chat anytime you feel like it. It's amazing how many students think that this is a good strategy. It isn't! Concentrate on making good relationships with your immediate colleagues and they will make sure that the people who need to know are aware of all your good work.

It's incredible to think but I have seen several work placement students get bored, think that the work they do is below them or spend their days on Facebook or Twitter in full view of the technical director. F1 is not a game, it is a highly competitive sport and a poor attitude will not sit well with your potential employer. If you are serious about making a career of this you need to grasp the opportunity and work hard. A sense of fun and social interaction is all part of it, but remember that you are on trial and a fantastic career is within your grasp.

Stiff competition means that you may well end up not getting the work placement that you really want. I didn't get my dream placement in F1 but that hasn't prevented me from getting the career that I craved. Formula 1 teams have structured work placement programmes but similar placements are possible in many other areas of motorsport too.

As I have mentioned several times one of the biggest mistakes you can make is to focus purely on Formula 1 to the exclusion of all else. By doing so you will miss out on many other good and relevant experiences elsewhere. MotoGP, World Rally Championship, NASCAR, IndyCar, Touring Cars etc. are all very high profile motorsports where work placements programs exist. They may not be advertised but you should contact as many teams, manufacturers and constructors as you possibly can and offer your services. The key point to remember is that the harder the placement is to find, the lower the competition for the place will be when you get there. It only takes one interested person and suddenly you have your foot in the door and your career in motorsport has begun. Experience gained here will be perfect to build up your CV for a time when you want to move across to Formula 1. Don't ignore opportunities just because they are not in F1, there are more open doors than you may think but you'll need to go looking for them.

3 F1 and how it fits within the motorsport industry

The focus of this book is rightly on Formula 1 as it is globally the most popular form of motorsport and considered to be the pinnacle of racing. Presumably the reason you are reading this is because you hope someday to be involved in Formula 1. F1 however is just of a part of a much larger motor racing industry which runs behind the scenes. The wider industry is an essential component in making the premier series function in the way that it does. Formula 1 makes the headlines but it is supported by a huge network of far less glamorous suppliers, feeder series and technology companies which are an essential part of the sport.

Much of what you see on television is dressed up in marketing and corporate decoration. The day to day business of motorsport can be somewhat different to the marketing exercise of the actual races and it is very important to understand and be knowledgeable about motorsport "beneath the skin" if you are serious about making it your career. Knowledge of how the industry works, which companies operate behind the scenes and who the influential players are can help you enormously in finding opportunities. It can also help your credibility too as a confident knowledge of wider industry will also convince potential employers that you know what you are talking about and take your career seriously.

In this chapter I hope to make you aware of just how big the motorsport industry really is, to show you where Formula 1 fits within that and how you can use the industry to help you reach your career goals. When motorsport comes up in general conversation, at least in Europe, invariably it is Formula 1 that people immediately think of. F1 has a huge history and has shared those times with some of the most famous car makers and racing teams of all time. Love it or hate it, it's hard to deny the influence and dominance that Formula 1 casts over global motorsport.

Even in the healthiest of times however there are only 13 teams who can compete in F1 and yet those teams have an influence that shapes and steers racing competition and technology across the world. There is much talk in the press about a money crisis in F1 but there is no doubt that the sport still generates colossal revenues. The budget of even a back marker F1 team means that significant cash is pumped back into the wider motorsport industry as the team manufactures, consults, invests and purchases from suppliers and support businesses. The money spent by an F1 team works its way across the wider industry putting food on the table for tens of thousands of business owners and employees.

The existence of a healthy and revenue generating Formula 1 grid is why the industry has been able to grow so big as a whole. The investment trickles down to smaller companies who provide services and technologies that F1 teams use in their pursuit of winning. Most F1 teams are in fact wholly dependent on their supplier networks to provide them with materials and components that they themselves cannot or do not need to source or manufacture.

Understanding this wider industry can be a key way to make it to Formula 1 as many supplier companies are in direct contact with the teams and working for them can allow you to build up a relationship with people who could potentially be offering you a job in the future. At key suppliers, you could even be designing parts of the car even though you don't work directly for the team. AP racing in Coventry and Brembo in Bergamo, Italy for example design the majority of the brake calipers and disc bells for the F1 grid between them, each to the team's unique size and specification. They also support those products by travelling to races, examining and servicing the units at the circuit. Employees of these companies can work in and contribute to F1 without working for one of the team's directly. By doing so they also establish a network of contacts within the paddock. When they need to or wish to they can draw upon those contacts and get a job in F1 from the inside. I know several people who have done precisely that.

Knowing the industry and how it works, which companies work with the teams and which have their respect gives you a massive edge of your competitors when it comes to finding openings and opportunities into F1. A central theme so far and one of the key messages I want to get over through this book is that you don't need and should not expect to get a job in F1 straight away. The industry exists as the way in, building up your experience, contacts and knowledge.

The idea that you can't get a job in F1 unless you have experience frustrates so many because they believe it to be an impassable barrier. How do you ever get the experience unless a team is willing to give you a job in the first place? Well the key thing to know and what so many others miss is that that experience doesn't have to be in F1 to be of interest to F1 teams. As anyone in the paddock will tell you, motor racing is motor racing and the same skills, motivations and attitudes that help you succeed in F1 can be gained in a whole host of racing supply companies throughout the industry not just in racing teams.

When the majority think about a job in F1 they only see the teams themselves and so limit their own chances and opportunities for a career. You however are going to be smarter than that. You now know that there is a whole industry out there that looks up to and works with Formula 1 teams and builds relationships and experience of the sport from below the surface. The biggest advantage you now have is that you will be one of the few who has this knowledge, one of the few that has looked beyond and one of the few that sees opportunity where other simply see a closed door. There are thousands queuing up for a job in F1 but the competition for places at companies who work *with* F1 teams is a mere fraction in comparison and this is where the secret of success lies. You will be able to use your knowledge of the industry to either work full time at an F1 supplier or to use that job as a stepping stone to a role at one of the teams in the future. This is exactly the route that I took and what many my colleagues did too. It's obvious when you think about it but easy to miss.

Congratulations. Having come this far you have now opened an enormous door to a wider world of motorsport that most people in your position simply do not know exists or do not understand how to take advantage of. Over the following paragraphs and chapters I will describe to you where to find openings and how to make the most of them. I will show you how to be one of the lucky ones. As we already know however, there is no such thing as luck and secrets. This is the unfair advantage that you now have over many people you are competing with for that job in F1.

The technology used in a modern Formula 1 car is staggering. The drive of competition and the substantial budgets of the bigger teams allow very specific technologies to be developed and these are often created with the assistance and knowledge of specialist suppliers from the motorsport and aerospace industries. F1 teams work very closely with supplier companies on car components such as brakes, wheels, tyres, dampers, fuel cells, gearboxes and electronics. These systems or some component parts of them will be designed and manufactured entirely by specialist outside suppliers to the team's specifications. This may or may not surprise you but even for the biggest teams it is not economic or sensible to invest in certain machines or technologies that do not offer them a unique advantage and therefore they rely upon the expertise of a supplier to provide them with that.

It may also surprise you to know that several teams do not in fact even manufacture their own chassis. Specialist companies such as EPM:technology provide capacity and expertise to produce moulds and carbon fibre layup to manufacture a Formula 1 monocoque to the desired shape and construction specified by the teams. If the team owns the design of the chassis then the technology to make it can be drawn in from outside.

Other companies such as Atlas and Formtech are used by teams to manufacture bodywork and aerodynamic upgrades that you see throughout the season. Using this outside capacity as well as their own composite manufacturing drastically reduces the delivery time of upgrades. This in turn allows them to produce more upgrades per season and increase their competitiveness. If you were to work in the laminating area of one of these companies you might be able to see bodywork and components from just about every team all in the same room at the same time. Confidentiality is key.

F1 teams are now much larger than they were in the past. In the 60's, an F1 team might have been 10 or 15 people typically, a bit larger for teams like Ferrari perhaps. In the 80's this number increased to more than 100 for a typical team but in the modern day even the smallest teams now have over 200 employees and some of the largest ones employ something approaching 1000.

As we have seen above however, it's still a fact that there is more work to do in F1 than the teams can cope with. There always will be. Metalwork machining capacity is also another area where teams rely heavily on outside companies to do their work and most, if not all will send out work to small high precision machining companies to manufacture uprights, suspension parts, even brackets and ballast. For those of you who are especially interested in making things, a job at one of these precision machining companies is an ideal route to working at an F1 team as you will almost certainly get involved in the manufacture of F1 car components. Not only that, you will have the advantage of having seen the designs of several different team's parts and be able to use that knowledge in your future role.

Facilities is another area where F1 teams rely on the suppliers from motorsport for expertise and assistance. The modern trend for simulators means that a market has opened for specialist companies to design and supply moving platform vehicle simulators and track mapping services to F1 and other high end motorsport teams. Ten or twenty years ago a similar market existed for 7 post rigs where a complete car is supported on various moving platforms to simulate road inputs such as bumps and kerbs as well as aerodynamic and cornering forces. Teams used these rigs to develop spring and damper settings before computer modelling was prevalent and experts from the companies that installed these machines were often poached to come and work at the teams to run and make the most of these facilities once fitted at the team's headquarters.

This poaching of expertise from suppliers is very common and it is easy to see why. If you use someone with specialist knowledge on contract basis you must pay by the hour and wait for them to become available. If you employ them you can have access to what they know virtually 24 hours a day. Working with them on contract beforehand you will have seen them work, get to know them and be sure that they are capable well before you commit to employing. Best of all, having an exclusive contract with them prevents them from contributing to the performance of a rival team. It is another example of the extended job interview process that we saw with work placements, where F1 teams get to know the people they employ before they are required to commit to hiring them.

Very few if any of the companies and types of suppliers that I have described above are household names and it would be difficult to find out about them without knowledge of the industry. They are simply not on most people's agenda. This is no bad thing for you however.

The age of the internet means that research is now much, much easier than it was before. Detailed research into the Formula 1 supplier network can be extremely lucrative as it can provide focused entry points into the industry which are not contested by other candidates in similar positions to yours. Resources such as the Motorsport Industry Association (MIA) and Autosport Directory list many suppliers in the industry which you can look up and learn about and then possibly contact for a job opportunity. Keeping an eye on these companies as well as the teams themselves gives you significantly more potential opportunities compared to limiting yourself and your outlook to F1 alone. A work placement at an F1 team is clearly everybody's goal but if you miss out you need a plan B. A work placement or job at a respected motorsport supplier will build your CV in the meantime and you will gain credibility through the experience. These companies might not be familiar to you but it's highly likely that they will be well respected by existing F1 engineers and that is the critical difference.

You should also think of the contacts and respect that Rich in my example earlier was able to build up without ever setting foot inside an F1 team factory. The competition for these places is minimal in comparison to those at the F1 teams themselves and if you are well qualified with a good range of experiences on your CV then the supplier companies will be fighting to get hold of you. Imagine that.

To get an idea of what kinds of companies you should be targeting you should seriously consider attending the Autosport International trade show which takes place at the Birmingham NEC in January each year. Many of the key suppliers in the industry will be present displaying their products and on the lookout for recruits. The Performance Racing Industry (PRI) in Indianapolis, USA is very similar and I am sure that there are equivalent racing trade shows in many other countries.

http://www.autosportinternational.com/trade/

The usual crowds will flock to the F1 team displays and driver interviews but the less glamorous trade stands will be virtually empty on public days. Staffed by employees looking to pass the time this is the ideal opportunity to walk up and have a chat, discuss what they do and hand over your CV and contact details. You rarely get as many face to face opportunities as this in a single place. Even at the racetrack people will be much busier and perhaps not have time to talk. At a trade show however you have the luxury of time and you should use it. Believe it or not I engaged myself in one such discussion many years ago and not only developed a relationship with company owner but sold him the idea that I could take part in the exhibitor's team kart race for him. The next day after the show I was racing against several professional racing and rally drivers including a very young version of David Coulthard. If you don't ask you don't get as they say.

By getting involved and working within the industry you will develop contacts, speak to colleagues who have worked at other suppliers, teams and even in Formula 1 who you can learn from and who can guide you on your way to a career in F1. Knowledge is key here and unless you get out there and get involved you will struggle to get started. As we have already seen, experience and opportunity are things that build stage by stage. Each experience that you gather can lead to something else and so on. Progress down this road can open further doors which you would not otherwise have come across. Each stage of your development gives you greater confidence and that feeling of belonging within the industry. Confidence shows and when it finally comes to the day when you get an interview in Formula 1 you will have the backing of not being a stranger to the industry and that feeling that you are already a motorsport person.

The next chapter describes an area of the industry which many of you will already be familiar. The so-called *racing ladder* is the route by which prospective racing drivers progress towards Formula 1 but we will be looking at whether it can also provide a way into the sport if you wish to work in Formula 1 from outside of the driver's cockpit.

4 The racing ladder

We spoke in the last chapter about Formula 1 being the pinnacle of motorsport and the existence of the racing ladder is testament to this as the analogy is often cited with Formula 1 being the top step on that ladder. The number of professional and amateur race series around the world means that the notion of a single route or ladder up to Formula 1 is not entirely true but most people can envisage a progression through the ranks where the cars become faster (and more expensive) at each stage and a driver build his experience against ever more talented rivals. To prove yourself worthy of a Formula 1 seat you need to build up a track record of success at each stage below it. Nobody can jump straight into a Grand Prix car and be competitive from nothing.

In the context of this book however I wanted to take the idea of the racing ladder and ask whether it also works for those wanting to make a career in the technical or marketing side of the sport. I have heard and read many so-called experts describing how *everyone* working in F1 has first proven themselves in Formula Ford, Formula 3 etc. but I can tell you that is simply not true.

Does it work and is it even necessary? Well, it depends on who you are and what you want to do but let's get into it and I'll try and describe my thoughts on the matter.

The idea of Formula 1 being at the top of a racing ladder suggests that you can start at the bottom and build up the skills and experiences that you need by competing at each stage on the way up. Each category should provide you with experiences and practice which you can then go on to use at a higher level and so on and so forth. The idea relies on the assumption that the job you do at each stage of the ladder is simply a more complicated or demanding version of the job that you did at the previous stage and that the lessons learnt can be put to good use.

For a racing driver, this is true as typically the performance of the cars at each stage of the ladder increases along with the length of races, the complexity of the cars and the setup options they offer. Each step on the ladder is however fundamentally the same as the previous one. For technical or marketing people on the other hand this progression does not exists in the same way because the business of Formula 1 is fundamentally very different to lower level motorsport categories. On the circuit, they appear closely related as we see a car and a driver but behind the scenes they operate on a completely different scale. Many of the jobs that you could do in Formula 1 simply do not exist in the lower categories of the racing ladder.

The fundamental difference between F1 and most race series is that in Formula 1 each team is a car constructor first and foremost and their racing team is only a small sub-section of a much bigger organisation. Most job roles within a Formula 1 team are concerned with either designing and manufacturing racing cars or generating the revenue required to run the business. Formula 1 teams employ hundreds of people in a wide variety of roles. In GP2, Formula 3 and most other series on the racing ladder the teams do not need to design or make their own cars because they are either a one-make series or the vehicles are purchased or hired from a specialist supplier. In those series, the teams consist only of the people who are needed to run the car at the racetrack plus a small number of administrative staff to run the business back at base. The concept of the business is quite different and so it is hard to compare between an F1 team and a team in the lower formulae. There are many job roles in F1 that simply do not exist in the lower categories and therefore the concept of the racing ladder does not work in quite the same way.

Imagine that you wish to become an aerodynamicist in Formula 1. In your dream job, you will be working in a state of the art wind tunnel developing wings and bodywork shapes that minimise drag and produce downforce to increase the car's cornering performance. A Formula 1 team constantly evolves its aerodynamic performance and so there is a constant turnover of ideas to test and a supporting team to design the parts, build a scale wind tunnel model and then manufacture the full-size components. To be an effective F1 aerodynamicist you need to develop knowledge and experience of how the airflow works around a racing car and to be able to analyse the data generated in the wind tunnel to drive the car's performance forward as quickly as possible.

If you work at a Formula 3 team however the job you would be doing would be very different to that which I have described above. Formula 3 cars use front and rear wings in the same way as Formula 1 cars do but the aerodynamic development happens in a very different way. Budgets in Formula 3 are tiny in comparison to a Formula 1 team (though hardly small) and they will not have the luxury of a wind tunnel and are in fact unlikely to have any kind of aerodynamic development program at all. The team which runs the car will consist mainly of mechanics to assembly the car and engineers to set it up at the track. An aerodynamicist in an F3 team would not be good use of that limited budget.

In this environment you can gain valuable experience of motorsport but it will not be particularly like the job that you will eventually do in Formula 1. It's a role that would be good to show your commitment and enthusiasm and develop your general understanding of motorsport. As a serious career development step however it is probably not going to serve you well. The fact that Formula 3, GP3 or even GP2 teams do not manufacture their own cars means that the experience you can gain for your target role is limited. Working with that team provides valuable learning but it is not necessarily the absolute best preparation you can get to learn to be an aerodynamicist. It is likely that for this job you can gain better and more relevant experience elsewhere.

Dallara produce what is currently the most popular chassis racing in Formula 3 at the time of writing and they are in direct competition with the other companies which manufacture alternative chassis for that category. Dallara do not run the racing teams themselves. They do however carry out aerodynamic development as part of their design process to ensure that their car performs better than their competitor's cars and that the top teams come to them to buy their cars rather than anyone else. In this environment, an aspiring Formula 1 aerodynamicist could find suitable training for their target job because they will be going through a very similar day to day process to develop a Formula 3 car as they will do in the future to develop an F1 car. It will be a much smaller team I would imagine but the process, aims and techniques will be very similar and so it would be very applicable and valuable training.

Working at Dallara or another chassis manufacturing company is not typically what people would consider to be working on the racing ladder. It is probably something closer to what I described in the previous chapter about working in the wider motorsport industry. When people say that you need to work your way up through the ranks to get to Formula 1 it is true but it is not necessarily via the same route as a budding racing driver might take. General experience of motorsport can benefit everyone but it is not necessary from a professional point of view for you to spend time in each Formula if it is not giving you direct experience of your target job role.

The racing ladder can be the ideal training ground for some as I am about to come on to but for most I would recommend that you consider exactly what it is in motorsport that you wish to do and then research as much as you can about the wider motorsport industry as well as the racing ladder before you decide where you should concentrate your efforts. For many people the supplier chains and less well known race car construction companies will be better training grounds for their skills than the race teams themselves.

It's tough call for many but one I want you to think about very carefully because despite what others (usually non-motor racing people) may tell you, it is not necessary to work in Formula Ford or other feeder categories to get a job in F1. Working in a lower formula can give you credibility but if you could gain better experience in another area of the industry then you should be wary of wasting your time and energy climbing ladders.

For all the discussion so far there is no doubt that the job seekers which can benefit from following the racing ladder the most is those who want to work trackside in Formula 1. The trackside group of an F1 team may be quite big but in essence it is only a larger scale version of the same group as you would find in any other race team on the racing ladder. Mechanics and race engineers are the 2 essential ingredients of any race team and in Formula 1 each car might have 4 dedicated engineers and as many as 7 or 8 mechanics. In clubman racing the driver might go racing on his/her own but at various stages of the day they will also be both mechanic and engineer carrying out the same tasks of checking the car over, cleaning it and altering the setup.

For many roles in a Formula 1 race team it is possible to find the equivalent position in a race team which is lower down the racing ladder. As you progress up that ladder, the number of roles and their similarity to the equivalent role in Formula 1 increases. The lessons and experience you gain by working your way up the ladder is much more relevant in this case and so the racing ladder comes into its own as a viable training ground and route into Formula 1.

A great number, if not most mechanics in Formula 1 will have previously worked as a mechanic in one or more different categories of racing before they started in F1. Of all the job roles in F1 this is the one where the racing ladder is most relevant. Some mechanics may have started out as apprentices straight into F1 and built up their experience in the team but the majority will have got there by working their way up as the cliché goes. A Formula Ford car may be considerably slower, less expensive and less complicated than a modern Grand Prix car but the discipline required to prepare it is almost exactly the same. The time pressure to turn around the car between heats or races is the same as you will find in Formula 1 and a meticulous attention to detail is just as important for the car's reliability. If you can excel in those lower Formulas then you are also likely to make a success of working in the premier category. There is no better training for being a race mechanic than being at the circuit.

The other way in which the racing ladder works for mechanics and other trackside personnel is through carrying reputation. People will (wrongly) tell you that you must know somebody on the inside to get you a job in Formula 1 but whilst this is blatantly untrue what you will find in motorsport is that it is a very open community and people talk. If you apply for a job at a new team it's highly likely that someone there will know someone else who has worked with you before. A quick phone call will be made or a brief chat in the pitlane will almost certainly follow and if you have made enemies or let others down then you can be sure that this reputation will get out. It's a business that works on reputation and so building up good working relationships in the lower formulas will pay dividends later when you seek to move up the ranks. You can't make a career just by knowing the right people but you can certainly damage it by crossing them.

For race engineers (and now data engineers too) the situation used to be very similar where you would work in lower formulas and build your experience into a Formula 1. This is however becoming increasingly *less* common as the Formula 1 job becomes more complex. If you were to look at the work history of the current crop of race engineers in Formula 1 you might find roughly a 50/50 split of those who have worked their way up and those who have graduated to that role from within their own teams. In modern Formula 1, a competent understanding of vehicle dynamics theory is a distinct advantage as it will allow the race engineer to discuss vehicle behaviour and setup with the boffins back at the factory and allow them to use that information and relationship to optimise the car. The discipline taught by an engineering degree is also much closer to the methodical practices which F1 teams use to run their cars at the circuit and so more and more race engineers have come from a theoretical vehicle dynamics background than was typical even 5 or 10 years ago. The advent of the data or performance engineer role (which is effectively a junior race engineer position) allows young and promising engineers from the factory to come and learn a trackside role by shadowing the senior race engineer. It is now also not uncommon for promising engineers to be loaned out to GP2 teams and such like to look after the protégé junior drivers that an F1 team has on its books so that they can grow together and learn their craft alongside the senior team.

In the past I would have said that to be a race engineer you should be looking to get your experience by working your way up the racing ladder in the same way that I have recommended for race mechanics. For engineers at least however, that is changing. Working in the lower formulas is still very valuable experience that can benefit your career but it is becoming increasingly common for factory based vehicle dynamics to be the training ground of choice. The racing ladder has its place but vehicle performance experience from the wider industry is now just as valuable and might be the quicker and more direct route. This is especially true as simulators become more sophisticated and the trackside environment can be recreated in a controlled environment back at the factory.

The advice in this chapter and the previous one is my best recommendation for how to get the right experience as you work your way up to Formula 1. What I will say however is to recommend that you are not too rigid in your plans and that you keep your eyes open for opportunity always. If an opening becomes available you should seriously consider taking it even if it is not quite what you anticipated because there is no best way or single route that you must take to reach your goals. Everyone is different and in many ways a varied experience or a different background might make you stand out and give you further opportunity that those who follow more conventional routes. As you may have read already at my website at www.jobinf1.com I ended up working for several years in CART (IndyCar) across in the US before I ever set foot in an F1 factory. That was never my intention but it was a fantastic experience which I don't regret in the slightest. It gave me a different outlook on motorsport that many of my F1 contemporaries lack.

Each step along the way will teach you something more and lead you closer to your goal. The next chapter is all about that process and is in my opinion perhaps the most important in section in this book. It is where I believe the true secrets of working in F1 lie. It describes the exact process that I and many current F1 people used to get their jobs and should you not be lucky enough to get a graduate job or work placement at one of the teams straightaway then you will need to pay particular attention.

5 Stepping stones - the simple secret

Over the previous chapters, we have seen how Formula 1 fits within a much larger motorsport industry and how suppliers and lower categories of racing both feed and follow the premier category. There is little doubt that Formula 1 is the most well-known form of motorsport in the world, especially outside of the US and it is normally the category of racing that people aspire to work in if they wish to make their career in the industry. I should know as I was one of them.

I also know however, from the phenomenal response to my blog at www.jobinf1.com that a huge number of other people want to work in F1 and they are desperate to find out how they can get a job there. There is a shortage of information to help. It is easy to become fixated on Formula 1 as the end goal, the ultimate target and fail to see that you need a route map to get there rather than make the leap in a single bound. The truth is that one of the best ways to get a job in F1 is to put your efforts into working in a totally different form of motorsport altogether and then worry about F1 later. The aim of this chapter is to explain exactly what I mean by this and why it might be the best piece of advice I can give you in this whole book.

F1 is beamed into our living rooms every few weeks and is covered by at least one major TV channel in most countries around the world. Its popularity as a sport is truly staggering. As the apparent pinnacle of motorsport many hundreds, thousands and tens of thousands of people would like to be part of Formula 1 and have that dream job that they see on television.

That popularity is however what causes the biggest problem for potential F1 people. The competition for jobs in F1 is huge and Formula 1 teams are bombarded with begging letters and poor quality applications from people who want to work in F1 just because they like watching it on television. Even if you are a genuinely good prospect for an F1 team it's very difficult to get noticed amongst all the poor-quality applications that they receive. As we know already, it becomes very difficult to get a foot on the ladder without motorsport experience.

The good news is however that it's very possible to separate yourself from this majority and work towards getting the experience that you need. You can also do it with a fraction of the competition from others that you would be up against trying to get into F1 at the very beginning. F1 might be your goal but looking slightly further afield at the very start can pay huge dividends. Opportunities for newcomers are limited in F1 but there are many more openings and ways into the industry if you just look a little way beyond the Formula 1 grid.

One of the biggest mistakes that Formula 1 job seekers make is getting stuck in the mindset of How do I get a job in F1? They believe that it's all or nothing and they can only see the gap between where they are now and where they want to be. One of the best pieces of advice I can give you is to change the question that you are asking to How do I get a job in motorsport, with an ultimate aim of getting to F1? If you do this it can open up your eyes to a far greater number of opportunities and the path to F1 from where you are now will become much clearer. The majority will miss the opportunities that exist simply because all they see is Formula 1. That may be sad for them but it's fantastic news for you and you should take full advantage of the open doors that it creates.

I've made no secret of the fact that I didn't get a job in F1 right away. Despite my best efforts, I had a very ordinary work experience year within my degree at an engineering consultancy. I graduated with a good degree but still struggled to get any response from F1 teams (I presume this sounds familiar to many people) and so I got an ordinary job at an ordinary company in the UK. It was well paid but far from the excitement and glamour of F1 and I hated every minute of it. Several of my university colleagues also had similar F1 ambitions to myself but once the pay cheque started to arrive each month from their steady jobs they soon became comfortable, forgot about their dream and have stuck at their careers in general engineering. For them, F1 was and still is just a dream.

I however decided I had to leave and set about on a mission to get into motorsport in whatever capacity I could. After a few months, I spotted an advert in an engineering magazine for a graduate engineer position at a small motorsport design company and so I decided to apply. This company didn't have a racing team and it certainly wasn't in Formula 1 but I had done my homework and knew that it was well regarded in the motorsport industry and would help me gain some valuable experience. It turns out that not many people applied for the role because it was not high profile but I threw everything at it and arrived at the interview well prepared. Although I did not have direct racing work experience this did not matter because the company wanted a young graduate rather than having to pay more for an experienced person from F1. My CV had some decent examples of experience of racing at hobby level and within my school projects and something must have clicked because I got the job. It was a small start but at last I had a toe (if not a whole foot) on the motorsport ladder. I left a big, well established company to go to a smaller, riskier one but it was the best move I have ever made in my career. Even though it was several more years before I first worked in F1, I've never looked back. It was a vital stepping stone to Formula 1.

I could tell you which company that was but to tell you the truth it no longer actually exists and even if it did that would be to miss the point entirely. By telling this story I don't mean that you should follow my footsteps exactly but I wanted to demonstrate that there are in fact many, many similar small companies involved in racing today. Any one of those companies can give you that start in your career and give you the understanding and grounding in motorsport that F1 teams crave. Those opportunities will not jump out at you like jobs advertised on an F1 team's website but that is perfect because when you do find them they will be less competitive and a well prepared candidate stands a very good chance of getting the role.

The key to me getting that first job in racing was not just that I had been gathering relevant outside experience and demonstrating my determination and keys skills but it was the fact that the job was so poorly contested compared to any high profile Formula 1 jobs that might be advertised. I would bet my bottom dollar that far less applicants went for that job than typically apply for unpaid work experience placements at Formula 1 teams. The odds were massively more in my favour going for that role than they were for getting a job in F1 straight out of university. The key to it had been research of the wider industry whilst others had thought only about Formula 1. Perhaps it was not the Monaco glamour which they sought but I used that first opportunity as the first of several stepping stones and ultimately the experience that I gained that I gained allowed me to apply to a Formula 1 team as an experienced motorsport engineer just a few short years later. The rest as they say is history.

Globally the motorsport industry is enormous. F1 is of course big business but it is still only a relatively small part of the industry. In earlier chapters, we discussed volunteering and getting experience in racing plus over the last few chapters we have examined how the racing industry works and what type of companies exist outside of F1. Almost all of this industry is relevant in some way to F1 and the way they relate to one another and work with each other means that Formula 1 is never too far away. The motorsport industry is very close knit and people move from team to team and company to company quite frequently. When you are on the outside this closed community seems to be a barrier to you but on this inside it can be an enormous help. Advice, knowledge and opportunity can be gained from all quarters.

The number of different ways that you can start your career in racing is huge in reality, if only you know where to look. Once through that door you are immediately part of the racing community and will learn more about the industry, work with experienced colleagues and see racing first hand and how it operates. With just a small amount of this experience you will lift yourself far above most F1 dreamers and put yourself in a very solid position to go after you dream position in Formula 1. Looking at your early career as the first steps towards a career in F1 is the best approach as you can hone your skills and further your knowledge with each stepping stone along the way. The first step is often the biggest one but once you are working in the industry, Formula 1 is typically only a few steps further down the road.

This book is about F1 and if you are reading it then it's highly likely that Formula 1 is also your ultimate career ambition. As we know, using the wider motorsport industry as a stepping stone to your goal is by far and away the most successful way to reach your target but the time you spend gathering experience and working towards your goals is not time lost. In fact, it should be far from it.

If you enjoy Formula 1 then you are almost certain to enjoy many other forms of motor racing too and a career in the World Endurance Championship, IndyCar, Touring Cars or Moto GP can be as much fun and as rewarding as a career in F1. You should be ready to embrace whatever opportunities come your way, make the most of them and enjoy the journey above all else because they can be some of the best times of your life. Formula 1 is a high pressure environment and many people who work in it think back to the early days of their careers in other areas of the industry with great fondness. Motorsport outside of F1 is often a great deal more fun, where you can get involved in more ways and in different roles much more easily. In my experience, engineers who have spent time in other series and worked with lesser budgets, resources and technology often have greater imagination and problem solving skills than those who have worked in F1 from the beginning. Formula 1 might be considered the pinnacle of the sport but it does not do everything well and lessons can be learned and brought into the sport from all kinds of other categories of racing. My recommendation to you is to seriously consider making racing outside of F1 your immediate goal. Use this time to absorb the experiences that it gives you before pursuing a career at a Formula 1 team. You will almost certainly find that you are ultimately a better engineer, marketer or mechanic for it.

I would hope that having worked in the business for nearly 2 decades I would have a reasonable knowledge of the motorsport industry, particularly in the UK. I'm not however familiar with every company, exactly what they do and how others in the industry view them. I'd love to name each company that might give you a useful stepping stone towards F1 but that would be a tall order and there would be new companies out there almost as soon as this book was published.

What I aim to do here is just to open your eyes a little bit, to try and pull you back from thinking only about F1 and to show you where your career path might begin. As always, it depends on exactly what it is that you want to achieve in your career but getting your foot on the ladder and being able to show an F1 team or another motorsport company that you have worked in the industry will straightaway put you far above the majority of F1 job seekers.

As a little bit of a starter, go away and research the following companies and see how they fit into the motorsport world and what motorsport series they support and contribute to. You might well have heard of some, others not but take it from me, this is just the tip of the iceberg and there are many more companies like these ones if you are willing to spend the time looking. Take a break, look away from F1 just for a while and see what exists around the outsides. As these past few chapters have been attempting to show you, you are far more likely to find an opening to start your career if you can get rid of that blinding F1 tunnel vision.

Prodrive
Hewland
Honda Performance Development
Pilbeam Racing Designs
HWA AG Engineering
Cosworth
Ilmor
BERU F1 systems
Xtrac
Dallara
McLaren Applied Technologies (MAT)
Lola
Wirth Research

As we have already mentioned, motorsport and especially Formula 1 are as much about marketing as they are about racing. The positive association and image that racing can generate is pushed hard by marketing people to maximise the return on the investment in technology and components that sponsors and manufacturers make in their racing programmes. The image of a racing team is somewhat fabricated and sold to the public as part of that marketing machine. Things are not always what they seem.

Manufacturer backed racing programmes are often where this illusionary smokescreen is put to best use. Car manufacturers clearly have very high levels of sophistication within their own companies, particularly in mass production and minimal cost but these technologies are often very different to those required by a racing programme. Low volume and high cost racing cars with rapid and reactionary development programmes are a big cultural diversion for car companies and many of them are not setup to compete against established teams despite their large budgets.

Instead of carrying out their racing programme by themselves therefore, large manufacturers will typically subcontract their racing programmes to smaller specialist racing companies who have the technology, know-how and reactive culture required to compete. What may appear to be a manufacturer team may in fact not be at all. Typically, it will be a run by a totally separate company and simply financed and branded as a manufacturer team.

Why does this matter? Well for you as a job seeker in the motorsport industry you need to know who exactly it is that you are trying to get a job with rather than waste your efforts pursuing the wrong company. Let's take the Mercedes F1 programme as perhaps the best current example of this. Most Mercedes road car research and production takes place in the parent company's home country of Germany as you might expect. You might imagine that the Formula 1 programme comes out of the same research and development budget and takes advantage of the vast knowledge of the thousands of Mercedes engineers who work in Stuttgart. This could not be further from the truth.

The mighty Mercedes Formula 1 team is in fact run out of 2 unremarkable villages in rural Northamptonshire in the UK. The engine facility and the chassis design centre are about 25 miles apart rather than on the same site because they both have their origins as independent racing companies which were created well before Mercedes decided it wanted to go Formula 1 racing. The chassis development facility has its origins as Reynard, a manufacturer that was successful in the 1990's and early 2000's producing all conquering IndyCar chassis. It bought the remnants of the famous Tyrrell F1 team and created British American Racing (BAR) which was ultimately bought by its engine supplier Honda to create that car company's racing effort. When Honda pulled out, it ran as Brawn GP before Mercedes swooped in and bank rolled the team into the guise that you see today. The name above the door may have changed but the DNA of the team is still that of a small racing company and many of the key staff will have remained throughout that changing period. If you get a job at Mercedes in Germany don't expect to see any real evidence of a Formula 1 racing programme.

The engine company has a very similar background. It was started by 2 employees of Cosworth and initially produced engines for Chevrolet in the US IndyCar series in the mid 1980's. Ilmor, as it was known at the time, started a fledgling F1 programme with back marker team Pacific F1. In the mid-1990's Chevrolet pulled out of IndyCar and their engines were rebranded under a sponsorship deal as a Mercedes IndyCar engine. The German company then decided to enter Formula 1 initially with Sauber and then famously with McLaren to form one of the longest lasting engine supply partnerships in the history of the sport. Mercedes decided to take an owning stake in Ilmor and rename it Mercedes AMG High Performance Powertrains which is the company you see today.

This kind of branding exercise is common throughout the sport. Subaru's ultra-successful rally programme with Colin McRae and the Impreza was run by Prodrive in Banbury who have also run Aston Martin Le Mans programmes and the Mini WRC campaign to name but two. Wirth Research were behind the original Virgin F1 team as well as running Honda sports prototypes in the American Le Mans series. Even Toyota's WEC cars are run by a specialist company in Germany with their origins in rallying. Toyota bought the company outright and brought with them a big company mentality to start their ill-fated F1 effort in 2002. Many believe that the operation would have been a great deal more successful if the parent company had just left them to it.

In short, you need to look beyond the branding to see exactly who is doing the work behind the scenes for any given racing programme and find where the development is being done. Uncovering that hidden layer of specialist motorsport companies is effectively what I did to find my first job in racing. So few people were competing for the job that I virtually walked straight in the door. That would be very rare at a Formula 1 team but it was my way in and ultimately led to the career that I have now.

I don't think working in any kind of motorsport is ever easy but in comparable terms this route is far more accessible and likely to yield results than simply knocking on the door of a Formula 1 team to beg and plead. There are opportunities to work in F1 straight from school or university and you should put 100% effort into preparing for work placements and apprenticeships but places are hotly contested and an element of luck is involved. If that does not work for you, your chances are far from over and working your way up the industry is a far more accessible and choice led way to control your career development. It is my opinion that people who have worked in other forms of racing prior to Formula 1 are far better prepared for life in the premier category as they will have worked through issues with realistic constraints rather than having a limitless budget to throw at problems without having to compromise or adapt. You might have to wait a little longer than others to get to Formula 1 but you will be with the majority in doing so and should not feel in any way that you are second tier or missing out. Going straight into F1 is quite unusual and not just for the super gifted or "best" candidates.

I hope this chapter has opened your eyes and broadened your horizons. What I have described over these past few pages is a world which is often unnoticed or unrecognised by aspiring F1 people but it is an everyday part of Formula 1 and all the motorsport industry. This is what working in F1 is all about and to understand this industry is to understand Formula 1 itself. I cannot get you a job in Formula 1, I wish I could, but that is just not possible. What I hope you have taken primarily from this book is an understanding of the differences between the reality and the fantasy of Formula 1. To be successful in getting the job you want you must focus on the reality and avoid the distractions and pitfalls that so many others fall into.

Much of racing is not glamorous at all and involves hard work in some very ordinary places and often at some unsociable hours. This is the reality but without going through that process and proving yourself you will find it very hard to be accepted by the racing community. If you are not interested in that then a job in F1 will forever stay a fantasy for you.

It might not be the racing that you see on the glamorous television coverage but this is the day to day reality and once you are a part of that world you will be accepted by the motorsport community. Once you are inside that community, Formula 1 is ever present and you will develop the experience and contacts that allow you to make that step up to your dream job. It's a simple process but one which is notoriously difficult to uncover or understand if you are on the outside. Formula 1 can be a huge lure because of the excitement that it portrays on television but it also blinds you to the reality. A little bit of research can go a long way to uncovering opportunities and unlocking that seemingly closed door to the motorsport world.

This step by step approach really is the key to a career in F1 and I hope that you can see how it increases the number of openings and opportunities for inexperienced people to get a foothold in motorsport. Each person is unique and their route to F1 might be different. Through experience and involvement, you will develop your own preferences and forge your own way to the pinnacle of the sport. Those first steps are often the most difficult but there are far more of them open to you that it first appears and reward awaits those are prepared to go that extra mile to find them.

6 How to fail and what NOT to do

So far, this part of the book has been concerned with strategies and research that can lead you to a career in Formula 1. I hope that by following them you will be well placed to fulfil your ambitions and earn your living by being involved with Formula 1.

Even if you follow my recommendations however there are still many pitfalls or myths that can affect your chances of success. To highlight some of these, this chapter will be all about what **NOT** to do.

The following pages contain a collection of common mistakes you can make in your pursuit of Formula 1 and the kind of things that you should avoid doing if you are to make a success of your bid. It is all too easy to fall into a trap and waste your efforts by pursuing the wrong strategies. I've made several of these mistakes myself and seen many of them in the applications of others. Hopefully by reading on you can save yourself some effort and potential embarrassment.

Writing speculative letters to F1 teams

It's a common scenario. You desperately want a job in F1 but don't know where to start. You do some quick internet searching, find the address of your favourite team and write a letter asking for a job. What have you got to lose?

You may have emphasised just how much you want it, how hard you work, how much you know about F1 already and how you'd be happy just to mop the floors to start with. Surely they'd give you a chance or at least an interview?

No.No, they won't. Not a chance. Don't waste your time. Your letter will go in the bin along with the many hundreds of similar begging letters that the teams get each year. It doesn't matter how good you are, begging letters never work and you should spend your time writing to weekend racers or your local club looking for voluntary work instead.

Suggest in applications that you watch all the races on television

Don't do this. The amount of television you watch and the number of magazines you read won't impress anyone and you should not expect it to. By all means watch TV and read magazines, in fact you should be doing those things but don't put it on your CV or in communication for job applications. The bar is much, much higher than this and teams expect *real* experience not just that gained from your armchair.

If you want to be appear professional and pro-active please don't mention your television viewing habits.

Think that you've done enough

I get many comments on my blog at jobinf1.com which list an achievement or exams results followed by the question "Will this be enough to get me a job in F1?" It's almost impossible for me to answer the question because there is no minimum standard or requirement for F1.

The point here is that it can never be enough. You must imagine F1 as a competition and consider that there will always be someone else out there doing more than you and that if you let them, they will be the one getting the job and not you.

Even if you have some solid experience behind you then you can always do more. I have many years direct F1 experience but if I want to further my career I know I need to do more. It never stops but one thing that you can be sure of is that if you do stop pushing then your chances will reduce very quickly indeed.

Believing that more and more education gives you more chance to get a job

This one is perhaps controversial but as has been a theme throughout this book, formal education is not enough for F1 and you should not rely on it. The best F1 people in my mind are those who have a decent mixture of formal education and real world experience.

Education is a measure of your knowledge and intelligence but so much of working life is down to initiative, drive and the ability to think outside the box. Only real life experience can develop and demonstrate these qualities, no amount of exams or certificates can bring the same balance.

Expecting too much too soon

I received an email from a young man earlier this year who was on the brink of giving up his dream of working in F1 as he had grown frustrated at the lack of opportunities. Amazingly he revealed that he had been a dedicated fan of F1 "for almost a year" and followed every race in detail. He had expected to get a job in F1 only a few short months after first considering the idea.

I was not surprised he had not yet found a job, he had barely had enough time to learn the driver's names let alone understand the business. If something is worth doing you should be prepared to work at it before you succeed. Hopefully it will not take an age but be prepared for the long haul otherwise you will almost certainly be disappointed.

Not looking beyond the hype & glamour

As you will now know, day to day F1 is not as glamorous as the television pictures might suggest as not it is not every day that we parade up and down the grid at Monaco. The real decisions and hard work take place in much more ordinary locations and with much more ordinary people. Television coverage attempts to make F1 appear to be something which it really is not.

The ability to look beyond this glamorous front will serve you well as you will spot opportunities that other miss as they are thinking only of meeting drivers and movie stars. If you expect F1 to be like Monaco every day of the week then you will be sorely disappointed and it's probably not the career for you.

Following salary in the short term rather than learning

As we will see in the next chapter you can be paid a vast amount of money in F1 but you should not expect to walk in on your first day and earn a fortune. Getting a job is only the start and you will then need to prove yourself worthy in a real working environment before you are suitably rewarded.

It may be that for the early years of your career you that you will be paid less than you could earn in other industries. Be patient and reward should come. If you throw the towel in and go and work somewhere else then you will almost certainly lose out in the long term. The choice is yours and you need to decide what is more important to you.

Quoting F1 tech blogs

The recent growth of online technology blogs and magazines has spread the interest in the technical side of the sport immensely. Craig Scarborough created the genre and now many have followed his lead with great success.

They can provide great insight into technical developments and are a valuable and free resource for you to expand your interest. I know several students who now write their own blog as a way of focussing their knowledge.

A word of warning however. If you read these blogs please do not take what they say as the absolute truth. Most technical developments on Formula 1 cars go unnoticed and even for those that are discussed, many are misinterpreted or misunderstood. Journalists in the popular media are not engineers (in general) and will not necessarily grasp the subtleties of a particular technology. Their job is to make good reading, not develop racing cars.

It will not impress a Formula 1 team if you write in your application how many blogs you read or use technical jargon learnt from magazines. Read them but be wary of relying on them too much.

Fixating on Formula 1 or worse still, particular teams

I spoke once with a young girl who wanted to study and go on to work in Formula 1. She sounded very confident and had done all the right things until she revealed that the only team she wanted to work for in F1 was McLaren and that she would not consider working at any other team even if offered.

Needless to say, this would make her chances of getting to F1 unnecessarily difficult. Everybody has their favourite team but you need to separate the fan inside you from the professional.

Ignoring grass roots motorsport

F1 is undoubtedly glamorous and very few forms of racing or other sports can generate an atmosphere to match. Lower formula and club racing are much more low key events and often take place in front of empty grandstands. Glamorous they are not but they are still vital feeders to the higher echelons of motorsport and they offer huge benefits to aspiring F1 job seekers.

It might not be what you dream of but some hard slog at unheard of teams or motorsport companies can set you up for a long-term career in the limelight. Time spent here might not impress your friends but it will impress potential employers. Choose wisely.

Exaggerating your experience

I get a great number of CV's in my inbox and every so often I get some that sound far too good to be true. "Technical Director" read one such recent application from a 22-year-old student when describing their current job role and work experience. Only further reading revealed that it was working on the restoration of a friend's road car.

Full marks for effort but there is no need to present yourself as something you are not. A humble and honest approach will be much better received.

Learning only from television and not from books or real life

The modern coverage of F1 is very high quality and gives insight into many aspects of how the drivers and teams operate, much of which was not available even 5 years ago. Good it may be but be wary that a TV show is exactly that and the broadcast is made to maximise the excitement of the race rather than be factually correct. If you do your learning from television rather than from real life it will be obvious to any experienced Formula 1 recruiter and not very impressive.

Books on the other hand tend to be much more accurate, especially those told by people who were there. I am a big fan of reading and learnt a great deal from absorbing books on racing and by prominent figures in the sport. Real life experience is ideal but you can learn a huge amount from the thoughts of others. See my blog as www.jobinf1.com for some books that I recommend.

Playing too safe and being afraid

I was very shy as a child and was reluctant to put myself into the limelight. Racing changed that as I was so determined to win that it forced me to do things I would otherwise have been too scared to do.

I once heard somebody recommend that you should do one thing each day that scares you. Whether it is introducing yourself to a team owner at a circuit, picking up the phone to speak to someone important or getting involved at a club where you know nobody, I find this motivator to be extremely useful. It may be daunting but remember that if you don't do it then someone else almost certainly will. Make sure you go the extra mile and make the most of opportunities. Step outside your comfort zone and go for it.

Looking at others with jealously instead of talking to them and learning from them

The myths and secrets that surround working in F1 are generally created by people who have missed out and are jealous of the success of others. There is no reason that you cannot succeed but if you assume that successful people have an unfair advantage or that you are being treated unfairly then you will almost certainly fail to achieve your dreams.

Rather than waste your energy being jealous, reach out to people who have made it to where you want to be. Learn from what they have done and how they did it. Social media and the internet make reaching out to people so much easier and you should take full advantage. Just don't expect Adrian Newey to answer your phone calls.

Appearing over confident

Reading a resume can often be done in just a few short seconds. Make a wrong move and recruiters will swiftly move your application to the "no good" pile.

One of the biggest turn offs is an applicant who acts with over confidence. I often see applications with bold claims such as "highly competent with all forms of data acquisition" or "able to use CAD to a very high standard". Don't do this.

I have used F1 standard data acquisition systems for years but know that I am a very amateur user compared to some. I have over a decade of design experience behind me but still struggle to use CAD as confidently as I want to. Be humble and accept that you can always learn more. The best engineers always ask questions and seek to learn and you should do the same. Making bold claims without the substance to back them up is a sure-fire way to convince a recruiter that you don't know what you are talking about and to put your application straight into the rubbish bin.

Giving up after a setback

As I have said many times, I did not make it into F1 very quickly. In fact, I was slower to get here than many others. I worked at several jobs before I finally worked for a Formula 1 team but each time I was learning, progressing and building experience. Along the way I had numerous rejections from teams, including I must say from the very team that I now work for...

It's a long game and you should not give up at the first setback. Your chance will come and when it does you will be ready to make the most of it. Nobody walks straight into this business without some hard work and some setbacks along the way so be prepared to be battle hardened.

Believing that school teaches you everything

I worked very hard at school but it wasn't until I got out into the world that I realised how tough life could be and how much more there was to learn. Luckily, I had my first taste of racing at a young age and learned to how to fend for myself and deal with people.

The most successful people in Formula 1 are not necessarily the cleverest, but typically they are driven, able to make decisions and think on their feet. These skills are not learnt in a textbook they are learnt from dealing with people and coping with new and different situations. Don't rely 100% on school to prepare you for work, you need to go out and learn from real people in real situations.

Failing to put yourself in the shoes of others

Business or any other transaction in life must be good for both sides and very few people will give away anything unless there is something in it for them. You may be desperate for an F1 team to give you a job but have you ever thought about what it is that they need from you? Nobody ever *gives* anyone a job, they offer it to them because they believe that this person can provide them with hard work and skills that can take their team or company forwards. The exchange must be a benefit to both sides.

If you go into any deal only thinking about what you want then you will struggle to succeed. Put yourself in the other person's shoes to imagine how you will come across and what that person needs from you at that time to give yourself the best chance of striking an agreement.

Looking too far ahead and missing what is in front of you

At age 10, Formula 1 looked a very long way away for me and I spent many an hour at school daydreaming about standing on the grid at Monaco alongside the likes of Nikki Lauda, Jody Sheckter and Alain Prost. It seemed impossible.

It wasn't until the last week of school that I discovered that my class teacher raced his 2-seater sports car as a hobby and had been a racing enthusiast all his life. He had a wealth of knowledge about motorsport and I spent several lunchtimes listening to him talk about racing and how he prepared his car. I learned more in those few short hours than I could have ever imagined.

Day dreaming of the ultimate prize is fine but I had almost missed what was right in front of me. It pays to talk to people and find likeminded individuals as they may be closer by than you think. As we have seen, knowledge and contacts build on top of one another and so it's important to always be on the lookout.

The list above is certainly not exhaustive but it gives you an idea of the kind of strategies that you need to avoid if you are to make the most of your time. I hope it can help you visualise the attitude that you need to be successful in Formula 1 or in life in general in my opinion. Much of it is common sense.

Making mistakes is all part of learning however and I am not afraid of saying that I made several of the mistakes I've outlined in this chapter. A lesson learnt the hard way is one that you never forget and often one which you will get the most out of. The idea of this chapter is not to make you scared of making mistakes, everybody does it, but simply to save you some time and keep you pointing in the right direction. The biggest mistake of all is not to try and to avoid situations where you might make even a small mistake. Being too cautious means that you might miss out altogether.

Whatever you do and whatever mistakes you make along the way, don't let those setbacks damage your confidence. Learn from what you have done and keep trying. The more you learn, the more you will have Formula 1 within your grasp.

Failing to try would be the biggest mistake of all.

7 What can I expect in return - salaries & benefits

We all know that F1 cars cost a lot of money and that many of the top F1 drivers live the playboy lifestyles of the rich and famous. How much does the average F1 team employee earn though? Do many F1 designers have apartments in Monaco and supermodel girlfriends/boyfriends?

In this chapter I wanted just to give you a flavour of what you might be able to expect as reward for your hard work getting to and working in F1. The job itself can be very rewarding but there are bills to be paid and teams need to compete for the best people with other companies and industries. Along with the usual crop of myths that surround Formula 1 I hear from many people that salaries in F1 are very poor and that you will be living on the poverty line in exchange for the privilege of working for the team. Is that really the truth?

Engineering is not known for being a high paying career. Despite there being a real shortage of qualified engineers in many European countries, the wider industry average salary is relatively modest in comparison to many other professional sectors. Most F1 employees work in engineering and so it should follow that salaries are also moderate at best. If so many people want to work in the sport then perhaps they are even below that modest average?

Formula 1 is exceptional in many ways however and the competitiveness of the sport means that F1 salaries are higher than the industry averages. As we will see you can earn a fortune in this job if you have the talent to excel.

So just how much can you earn as an F1 engineer? Well, if your name happens to be Adrian Newey then you can command a multi-million dollar wage comparable to or better than half the drivers on the grid. If you have another name however then you could earn anywhere from Mr. Newey s salary all the way back to the minimum wage. It's all about your worth or value to the team and that is where much of the confusion arises. The variation is enormous but for good reason.

Formula 1 is a capitalist driven business. The rewards for success are large but the penalties for failure are very harsh indeed. For teams the rewards are heavily biased towards the front of the grid.

Salaries for engineers are very similar in that the very top engineers can earn telephone number wages but very junior employees may be paid comparatively poorly. There is no pay structure or prescribed pay scales in F1, every employee is paid whatever they can negotiate and in some cases there may be a large difference in salary between 2 similar people doing a similar job. This puts many people off working in the business but I personally believe that this right for Formula 1 and is the way to get the best out of people.

Some may disagree with that but as I said earlier, F1 is an exceptional business and exceptional people need to feel that they will be rewarded for going the extra mile.

It's important to understand that this isn't about fairness or equality, nothing in F1 is about equality. It is about reflecting a person s value to a team and how hard they would be to replace were they to quit and go to another team. If you are reading this blog you will probably know that getting started in an F1 career is very difficult because a great many people want to work in the sport and are willing to do so for little or no financial reward. At this end of the market, teams have the luxury of being able to pick the best people and have little motivation to pay high salaries if they can easily replace them with another willing volunteer. If you have limited experience then you should not expect a high salary until you have proven yourself and built up your value.

In truth, starting salaries for graduates in F1 are decent and comparable with other engineering sectors. There is no pay structure in most teams and as team policies vary it is difficult to put a single number to it but I would suggest that the average graduate engineer or one with only a year or so of work experience would earn somewhere between £20,000 and £30,000 depending on the position and their qualifications.

As your experience increases however, so does your value to the team and to prevent you leaving and taking what you have learnt to a competitor you will quickly get a pay rise. If you do your job well and show promise then that reward may be significant. Middle ranking engineers may earn considerably more than a junior engineer after just a few years of work. It is a case of working hard and being patient in the early years of your career even if you feel that initially you could earn more elsewhere. In F1 you need to prove yourself first and then the reward will follow. The opportunity is there to far exceed income in more ordinary industries where pay scales and equality limit an individual's potential.

It's a cliché but part of the reward of working in F1 is the involvement in the sport and enjoying what you do and so even if you don't earn Newey money then there is still a lot to be taken from a career in F1. If you do it just for the money then it is unlikely that you will enjoy it or stick at it in the long term. If that is your motivation then you might want to avoid working out how much you earn on a per hour basis. That said, I still have those days where I look around and realise that I am spending my day working on the world's most advanced racing cars and need to pinch myself. Compared to what many people must do to earn a living it's sometimes hard to believe.

As your career develops you should become increasingly valuable to your team. One of the great things about the pace of F1 is that you will be exposed to a vast amount more in your early years in comparison to normal industries. You might work on brakes one week and then steering the next or develop front wings, floors and barge boards all in the same year. You might be the only person in the team with significant experience of some particular aspect of the car and so if you leave, the team stands to lose that knowledge and expertise. Suddenly your negotiating position can be very strong.

Many senior engineers are on multi-year contracts with their teams to ensure that they do not leave and take valuable information with them. Salary ranges for these types of people range are several times those of the junior engineers particularly those with a unique expertise or experience. With such reward however you will need to take on increased responsibility and handle the pressure of high expectation. Senior engineers are typically responsible for complex areas of the car such as chassis structure, suspension design or aerodynamic performance of the front or rear wing assemblies. The success and failure of those projects must be carried by the individual and so the stakes are high.

After many years of service and experience you may be able to move towards managerial roles such as a department head or potentially chief designer or chief aerodynamicist. At this point, there is certainly no form guide for salaries but safe to say there are a lot of *very* nice cars in the car parks of most F1 teams. To reach this level you need to be a very capable individual who can stay on top of several different projects and issues under pressure. This is the big time of Formula 1 and many engineers in upper reaches of this category are now household names. The role of technical director is probably still the pinnacle of F1 engineering, taking overall responsibility for aerodynamics, track performance and car design. Salaries of these people are seldom revealed but during Williams F1's flotation on the stock market in 2009, the IPO prospectus showed that the then technical director Sam Michael's income was £469,000 per annum. You can see this for yourself at the following link:

*http://www.williamsf1.com/Documents/Investors/
211022035_110207_Prospectus_FSA_final_Total_Internet.pdf*

This is still likely to be short of salary of the technical directors of the bigger teams such as McLaren, Red Bull and Mercedes but clearly it is still a very substantial sum. I am sure that most of us would be very happy to be rewarded in such a way and outside of investment banking or company ownership I don't think there are many jobs that have this earning potential.

If you reach those heights in your career then you are probably talented and confident enough not to be reading this book. Good luck and think about the start I gave you! As with everything in motorsport, reward goes to those that work hard and commit to their goals. Working in F1 is not an easy path to riches and is not for people who expect a 9 to 5 lifestyle but the sky is the limit if you have the ambition.

Winning in F1 comes with massive reward. We have discussed salaries already but there is another form of compensation that is offered in return for success in this sport. Performance related pay schemes are almost universal and can often top up already attractive salaries should you and your team have a successful season.

The exposure, positive association and press coverage of winning are worth a fortune to the team owner and sponsors. In a good season, win bonuses can amount to many thousands of dollars and form huge percentages of an employee s salary. In F1 everyone shares in success which makes winning an even more attractive goal from for the whole team.

In 2014, it has been well documented that every member of the Mercedes F1 team was given a £10,000 bonus over and above their normal salary as a thank you for winning the constructor's championship. This was widely reported by the press having been leaked out by team members. Such reward seems very lavish but Mercedes as a car company clearly felt that they stood to gain substantially more than this in car sales because of that success and so were happy to hand out the reward as a thank you gift for their tirelessly hard working staff. The payment was made equally from Technical Director to cleaners and van drivers which showed great values from the parent company and management.

This type of arrangement is very typical in Formula 1 as the teams seek to incentivise their employees and give them a share in the spoils of winning. Mercedes AMG High Performance Powertrains (MAHPP) might be a separate company, producing the immensely successful hybrid power units that propelled the Mercedes cars to that championship but the same parent company was paying the bills and their win bonus too. MAHPP employees did not get the same championship bonus as their car constructor colleagues but received a win & podium related bonus on a race by race basis. Not only do they get that bonus for the factory Mercedes cars but they were also rewarded for the results of Mercedes customer teams Williams, McLaren and Force India. When you consider how good a season Williams had in particular, that means that employees of MAHPP had been getting bonuses for 1st, 2nd & 3rd in many of the races in the second half of the season. I don't know the numbers but I'll bet it's no small addition to their annual salary.

Every team has some kind of bonus or points incentive, it's a good way of letting the employees share in the spoils and motivating them to push the team forward. For the back marker teams, just a handful of points is a massive bonus and would probably bring a decent reward for the working people in those outfits. Whilst every team owner would dearly love to score a massive haul of points, they must be careful because a generous points bonus scheme dreamt up when the team was unlikely to score more than a handful of points in the whole year can severely back fire if the team s performance suddenly takes a significant step upwards. He or she may find themselves paying out dearly when years of dismal poor performance suddenly changes to regular podium places and 2 car points finishes.

Money might be tight at the lower end of the grid but in true winner takes all style, the rewards at the front are higher than ever.

Not only can you aim to receive a decent salary in Formula 1 but at most teams there are also many sponsorship related deals that can allow you to purchase sponsor products at heavily discounted prices. Engine manufacturers such as Mercedes, Renault and Fiat(Ferrari) offer car schemes to employees allowing everyone to drive a brand new car if they choose to do so. I don't know if the Fiat deal extends to Ferraris or Maseratis but I am sure there is some kind of benefit if you find yourself rich enough to afford one.

Sunglasses, sportswear, bikes, energy drinks, mobile phones, computers, toiletries you name it there are a discount on most things and companies and suppliers fight amongst themselves to supply items to teams and get them to wear their products in the pit lane and on television. Oakley sunglasses famously provide their products at an enormous discount to motorsport employees all over the world as they know very well how many people will be visible on television wearing them on the gird and around the paddock. This is effectively endorsing their product with the F1 image.

Bernie Ecclestone and FOM are generally kind enough (believe it or not) to provide free tickets to the teams for workers to go and see their products racing on circuit and I have probably been to more Grand Prix for free over the years than I have ever had to pay for. It's a perk for sure.

In testing I have watched the action from marshal posts, the pitlane entrance, pitwall and other money can't buy viewing spots. It's amazing what a team shirt and a paddock pass can get you in terms of access at a Formula 1 circuit and something that not even VIP sponsors get to see. You are not really watching Formula 1 if you cannot feel the heat of the car and the burning smell of the brakes as it passes by.

Can you imagine getting paid to sit in a Formula 1 car? I've lost count of how many different cars I have sat in in the name of work. That's something I dreamt of at school. I've taken part in pitstop practice, driven simulators, fired up V10 engines, been driven by world champions, lapped famous circuits in hire cars, run up Eau Rouge and had lunch with team principals. I must pinch myself sometimes but I'm not trying to be boastful here, these types of experience are very normal in motorsport. It's where it ceases to be a run of the mill job and becomes a racing fan's playground.

It's a small thing but pride in what you do can makes a big difference to your personal confidence and contentment. Small talk and conversation in social situations inevitably lead to you being asked what you do for a living. An answer such as "I work in insurance" or "I'm a solicitor" rarely provokes interest in the opposing party. If you reply "I work in Formula 1" however it is amazing how strong a reaction your answer can create from other people. Fan or not, most people will want to know more and you can often be caught discussing Formula 1 with strangers in all sorts of situations.

Many people I meet are embarrassed about what they do for a living but it's a big part of what you do and who you are. People inevitably judge you on it (rightly or wrongly) and to be proud and satisfied by what you do for a living can contribute to your happiness and well-being. Nine to five is a long time to hate what you do and coming home satisfied with what you have done with your day is the way that it should be. Seeing your car achieving success on track and beamed into your home via television is a tremendous feeling and very motivating. It's good for the soul.

In short, working in Formula 1 has some amazing benefits and allows a comfortable and fulfilling lifestyle both at work and at home. The long hours sometimes mean that sacrifices must be made but you will be rewarded for what you put in. Whilst you are unlikely to be buying a Ferrari and an apartment in Monaco any time soon you get to share in an incredible world of sport that is quite unlike most day jobs and take home your share of the spoils when success comes.

Most people that I know in this industry would rather work in Formula 1 than any other profession and I don't think that many occupations can live up to it unless you happen to be talented enough to sit in the driver's seat yourself. It's worth every bit of the effort to get there and I hope that through this book I can help you share those same experiences.

8 Ready for Formula 1

The ideas I have described in this book are not complicated and can be followed by almost anyone. I cannot guarantee you a job in Formula 1 but I hope I can set you on your way. By broadening your understanding of the real industry behind Formula 1 piece by piece you too can have the opportunity to work on these exotic and challenging machines and potentially travel the world and take part in Grand Prix racing at its very heart. It is a realistic proposition and not just a fantasy.

I hope that this book has encouraged you and given you motivation to follow your goals. Formula 1 is often misunderstood and others may try and convince you that it is a dangerous world or that it is corrupt and out of reach. Think carefully when you consider the advice of others and ask what their experiences are. Normally you will find that the people who confidently tell you these things have never worked in Formula 1 and know little if anything about the realities of racing. Needless to say, you should ignore them.

They say that you are a product of the people who you surround yourself with and I think this is very true. If you get the opportunity to follow and learn from real racing people you will inevitably absorb both their knowledge but also their enthusiasm and optimism. A huge part of this book has been about getting out there and getting on and meeting people. If you take one lesson from me it should be to push yourself outside of school, even in an environment where you are initially uncomfortable. If you don't ask, you will not get and looking back on the story of Rich and Joe we saw how quickly the lives of two people of very similar ability can diverge if only one of them is willing to go out and make opportunity happen.

I cannot make a career in Formula 1 happen for you but I hope over these past pages and chapters I have shown you how it is possible. I hope now that you can see how the myths, mysteries and the apparent secrecy that is normally perceived to surround the sport can be broken down and understood. The opportunities are there and you should now be equipped to find them and exploit them rather than let them pass you by. Competing in racing is all about

out thinking the opposition and getting a job in the industry is the same. You need to push yourself, search harder and come back stronger after setbacks. This is the only way to win.

I trust that this book has given you a head start and shown you the direction that you should be heading in. For many of you, a rewarding career in the top flight of motorsport might now only be a few steps away and you are well on your way to fulfilling your dreams. A Grand Prix victory may be within your grasp but the rest is now up to you.

I wish you every bit of luck, success and fulfilment and sincerely hope that I will be able to welcome you into the Formula 1 paddock soon.

If you have enjoyed this book and found it useful or interesting I would very much appreciate your feedback. Independent authors such as myself struggle to be found by members of the public as we do not have the marketing power of a large publisher. Reader reviews can help enormously to increase visibility and allow others to discover the content. If you could spare a moment, I would be <u>very grateful</u> for an honest review on Amazon.

Part 6 : Essential Resources

Resources

In this final part of the book I wanted to list easy to find and read resources that you can use to focus your efforts and search for those all important opportunities to break into motorsport.

Please check out www.jobinf1.com/book-resources for additions to this list as and when they are added so that I can keep it up to date and relevant. The following should be a good start and give you plenty of additional reading and ideas.

The Teams

RED BULL RACING

Red Bull Racing Bradbourne Drive Tilbrook Milton Keynes MK7 8BJ

United Kingdom

http://www.infiniti-redbullracing.com

@redbull

SCUDERIA FERRARI

Ferrari SpA Via Abetone Inferiore n. 4 I-41053 Maranello (MO) Italy

http://formula1.ferrari.com

@ScuderiaFerrari

MCLAREN

McLaren Technology Centre Chertsey Road Woking Surrey

GU21 4YH England

http://www.mclaren.com

@MclarenF1

RENAULT F1

Whiteways Technical Centre, Enstone, Chipping Norton Oxfordshire

OX7 4EE

https://www.renaultsport.com/

@RenaultSportF1

MERCEDES

Mercedes AMG Petronas Formula One Team Operations Centre Brackley NN13 7BD

Northamptonshire United Kingdom

http://www.mercedesamgf1.com

@MercedesAMGF1

SAUBER

Sauber Motorsport AG Wildbachstrasse 9 CH-8340 Hinwil

Switzerland

http://www.sauberf1team.com

@SauberF1Team

FORCE INDIA

Sahara Force India Formula One Team, Dadford Road, Silverstone, Northamptonshire

NN12 8TJ United Kingdom

http://www.forceindiaf1.com

@ForceIndiaF1

WILLIAMS

Williams F1, Grove Wantage Oxfordshire OX12 0DQ United Kingdom

http://www.williamsf1.com

@WilliamsRacing

TORRO ROSSO

Scuderia Toro Rosso Via Spallanzani, 21 48018 Faenza (RA) Italy

http://www.scuderiatororosso.com

@tororossospy

HAAS F1

HaasF1 (UK) Overthorpe Road Banbury Oxfordshire OX16 4PN

HaasF1 Haas Way Kannapolis NC 28081 UNITED STATES

https://www.haasf1team.com

@HaasF1Team

The Engine Suppliers

MERCEDES AMG HIGH PERFORMANCE POWERTRAINS

Mercedes (MAHPP) Morgan Drive Brixworth Northamptonshire NN6 9GZ

http://www.mercedes-amg-hpp.com/

SCUDERIA FERRARI

Ferrari SpA Via Abetone Inferiore n. 4 I-41053 Maranello (MO) Italy

RENAULT SPORT

Renault Sport SA 1 Avenue du President Kennedy 91170 Viry-Chatillon France

http://www.renaultsportf1.com/

@RenaultSportF1

HONDA F1

Honda F1 R&D Sakura Tochigi Japan

Honda F1 (UK) Mugen Technical Centre Snowdon Drive Winterhill Milton Keynes MK6 1AP United Kingdom

http://en.hondaracingf1.com

@HondaRacingF1

The Motorsport Industry

In many of the chapters of this book, but in Part 5 in particular I have suggested that the best way to get into Formula 1 is to work your way into the premier category via one of the many supplier or non-F1 related companies that make up the wider motorsport industry. I gave several examples of companies that offer these kinds of stepping stone opportunities but the industry is so large that it would be impossible for me to list every relevant company in this book.

Luckily there are several sources which have done this for me and the following is a list of the best and most appropriate of those:

Autosport Magazine Directory

http://business-directory.autosport.com

The Motorsport Industry Association (UK)

http://www.the-mia.com/The-Industry

Brits on Pole

http://www.britsonpole.com/in-depth/locations-of-british-motorsports-companies

Racecar Engineering Magazine

http://www.racecar-engineering.com/directory/

Career Advice

One of my main motivations for writing this book was the need to bring together in a single place a definitive career guide for Formula 1 as so much poor or unqualified advice exists across the internet and school system. That is not to say that none of the existing advice is good or worthwhile however, it certainly is. The following resources are webpages that I consider good to follow and an accurate portrayal of the industry:

The Motorsport Industry Association

http://www.the-mia.com/assets/What_do_I_need_for_a_career_in_Motorsport.pdf

Renault F1 - "I want to be" series

https://www.renaultsport.com/-Carriere-.html

F1 Elvis - honest advice from an ex-McLaren mechanic

http://f1elvis.com/2015/03/12/getting-into-f1/

Go Motorsport - general advice about getting involved

http://www.gomotorsport.net

Lime Rock Park - a small track in Connecticut but site has some of the best advice I've seen

http://www.limerock.com/

Or http://jobinf1.com/2014/10/20/how-to-get-a-job-in-motorsports-by-the-people-who-work-there/

Job in F1 - my site but a host of extra content not covered in this book

http://jobinf1.com

How to get a job in F1 - Mercedes F1 video

http://youtu.be/Gk0e_AoV2Zo

HOW TO GET A JOB IN GRAND PRIX RACING

What you need to do to get a job in F1 - Dominic Harlow

http://youtu.be/Y2kmLYrGa2Y

Working in F1 - ING Renault F1

http://youtu.be/fFn1l0WDkx4

In addition to the above, many of the team websites have case studies and interviews with members of staff which can be invaluable. I do a lot of internet research into F1 careers and tweet links to good articles via my Twitter account @Work_in_f1.

Job Listings

The official team websites are generally the best places to go for current vacancies but several other sites and resources carry relevant listings. It is worth making a weekly habit of checking them, if nothing else it will give you an idea of what is around and what kind of roles come up, even if you don't apply.

Don't rely on the general sites 100% though. Some of the best non-F1 opportunities will show up only on the individual company websites and will be far less contested than well advertised ones. You should be researching the industry and have a long list of companies and team to contact and follow and be checking their recruitment pages directly.

Autosport Magazine

http://motorsport-jobs.autosport.com @motorsport_jobs

Race Staff

http://www.racestaff.com

Recruitment in Motorsport (RIMS)

http://www.recruitmentinmotorsport.co.uk

TXM Recruitment

http://www.txmrecruit.co.uk/jobs/red-bull-technology/

LinkedIn

https://uk.linkedin.com/job/motorsport-jobs/

RICHARD LADBROOKE

People to follow on Twitter

The following list is a mixture of informative organisations and F1 people who I follow on Twitter for their insight into the sport

@BMMC_UK @Motorsport_Jobs @myweekendwarrior @MarkCox @NC4Motorsport @TreshamCollege @Benjiani79 @sandra_phoenix @GPPaddockPass @Autosport_Show @NatSKA_Karting @gomotorsport @Seabs @Resta_Simone @GuardianCareers @JPLatham7 @StudentMSport

@rachelfurn @FormulaMoney @txmrecruit @MSAUK @lukeroberts141 @AlanPermane @Race_Staff @BLOODHOUND_SSC @SilverstoneUTC @F1inSchoolsHQ @f1elvis @F1nomics @Greenpowertrust @xevipujolar @theBUKC @_markgallagher

RICHARD LADBROOKE

Printed in Great Britain
by Amazon